HEY DAD!
Are We There Yet?
One Man's Tireless Search for the
Perfect Family Vacation

Harold B. Smith

NAVPRESS
BRINGING TRUTH TO LIFE
NavPress Publishing Group
P.O. Box 35001, Colorado Springs, Colorado 80935

3. 00

The Navigators is an international Christian organization. Jesus Christ gave His followers the Great Commission to go and make disciples (Matthew 28:19). The aim of The Navigators is to help fulfill that commission by multiplying laborers for Christ in every nation.

NavPress is the publishing ministry of The Navigators. NavPress publications are tools to help Christians grow. Although publications alone cannot make disciples or change lives, they can help believers learn biblical discipleship, and apply what they learn to their lives and ministries.

© 1994 by Harold B. Smith

All rights reserved. No part of this publication may be reproduced in any form without written permission from NavPress, P.O. Box 35001, Colorado Springs, CO 80935.

Library of Congress Catalog Card Number: 93-48495
ISBN 08910-97732

Cover illustration: Danielle Jones
Interior illustrations: John McPherson

Smith, Harold (Harold B.)
    Hey dad, are we there yet? : one man's tireless search for the perfect family vacation / Harold B. Smith.
        p.   cm.
    ISBN 0-89109-773-2
    1. Vacations—Humor. 2. Family life—Humor. I. Title.
PN6231.V2S65   1994
818'.5407—dc20   93-48495
                                     CIP

Printed in the United States of America

FOR A FREE CATALOG OF
NAVPRESS BOOKS & BIBLE STUDIES,
CALL 1-800-366-7788 (USA)
or 1-416-499-4615 (CANADA)

Your Itinerary

1   We're the Smiths, and We Can Do
Anything!   7

SECTION ONE: DO YOU, JUDY, TAKE THIS ROAD MAP?

2   I Left My Lunch in San Francisco   15
3   "Dear Mother Nature"   25
4   All This for a Beach Vacation?   31
5   Next Time, We Drive to Hawaii!   37
6   Adventures in Undersea Camping   43
7   A Good Night's Rest Is Hard to Find   51
8   The Seoul of Miss Manners   59
9   How Not to Sail a Boat   65
10   Watch It Mister, That's My Wife   71
11   The "Real" Differences Between
Men and Women   77

SECTION TWO: LIKE FATHER, LIKE SONS

12   Are We There Yet?   87
13   My Children, The Road Hazards   93
14   So That's Why They're Called "Badlands"   99
15   Attack of the Killer Scorpion   105
16   What I Did on My Summer Vacation   111
17   Wanted: Souvenirs—Dead or Alive   117
18   Just Say "Cheese"   123
19   Like Father, Like Sons   129
20   Reunion of the Road Warriors   135

*This book is dedicated to
the "original" Road Warrior and Navigator,
my parents,
Harold and Dorothy Smith*

1

We're the Smiths, and We Can Do Anything!

Remember the Chevy Chase movie *Summer Vacation*? Chevy Chase, as beleaguered dad Clark Griswold, took his family on the holiday road, determined to "make memories." All along their cross-country nightmare they encountered road construction, tourist traps, car trouble, crooked mechanics, mooching relatives, and a death in the family. (This last happens in the back seat of their station wagon.)

For at least ten of my first eighteen summers, I lived that movie (except for the back-seat demise).

◆ I remember the wonder my parents desperately tried to impress upon my little sister and me as they pointed out the two-millionth example of native flora and fauna. ("Hey, kids, look. Another chipmunk!")

◆ I remember holding my bladder "just until the next rest area"—which by some cosmic oversight was always another two hours away.

◆ And I remember my father's sense of near-holy quest as he mapped out our vacations and confronted the

7

challenges therein. Each stop was calculated. Each expense predetermined. Three thousand miles in three days! No problem. We're the Smiths, and we can do anything!

But our family vacations not only gave me the opportunity to see my country and my world, they also presented a context in which to see friends and family in a new light. For example, for three weeks every year my dad was no longer Harold B. Smith, Ford Motor engineer, deacon, and disciplinarian, but Harold B. Smith, Road Warrior. Whether he was behind the wheel of his bronze '55 Ford or a steel-blue '59 Thunderbird (my favorite), my dad would take on all detours and road construction, confidently drive over hill and dale, and generally arrive at each night's destination at his preordained time.

His faithful companion, Mom, pretty much did on the road what she did at home—namely, keep her three kids (me, my sister, and my dad) happy and out of each other's hair. But she was also the keeper of the maps, and therefore responsible for keeping her Road Warrior husband on the right path. Though a sometimes harrowing responsibility ("What do you mean we should have turned left 234 miles back, Dorothy?"), Mom handled the navigating with ample humor and grace.

Humor and grace played a critical role in our facing up to the multiple "surprises" that stalked every one of our long-distance outings. Surprises that could hardly be characterized as "fun" while we were living them. But surprises that, with every telling and retelling, have helped shape our vacation lore (not to mention strengthen our family's gift of exaggeration).

My first vacation surprise came during my first vacation experience—Delray Beach, Florida, 1955. The Smiths—Road Warrior, Navigator, Little Sister, and Yours Truly—arrived just when Hurricane Connie was turning Florida's Atlantic Coast shoreline into a debris-strewn disaster area. (Vacation Law #1: Weather is never a respecter of vacations.) Waves fifteen and twenty feet high were crashing onto the beach, and hurricane winds shook the walls and windows of our oceanfront apartment.

I was bummed—disappointed that the "big swimming pool" just outside our front door was "closed until further notice."

I don't know if it's genetic, but there is a vacation mind-set born of every Smith: You play with the hand you're dealt. Tidal waves keeping you from leisurely floating on your favorite air mattress? So what! Go for it! Just expect to be thrown off your air mattress a little more often than usual.

And so, determined little Road Warrior wannabe that I was (and with dad, mom, and sis nowhere to be found), I left to catch a wave.

What happened as I approached the shoreline occurred so quickly I had no time to be scared—or even to run. A huge wave— witnesses say a fifteen-footer, I say a ninety-five-footer—swept over me and, in an instant, pulled me into the ocean maelstrom.

So this is vacation, I thought, as I made eye contact with a passing sea bass. (It was the beginning of my negative beach bias.) But almost as quickly as I had been set adrift on the stormy sea, I was tossed back toward shore—and into the arms of my dad who was walking the beach in search of the "treasures" Connie might be giving up.

After a joyous and rather tearful reunion in my father's arms (Vacation Law #2: Dads are always in control—or at least they seem to be), Dad sternly looked down at me and asked what this near-death experience had taught me.

Don't quote me, but I'm sure I answered: "Next year, Dad, we go West!"

Humor and grace also carried us through another surprise legacy-builder—an unnerving escapade that occurred in, of all places, our beloved West. I say "beloved" because: (1) the West is a rugged and rocky haven in which all true Road Warriors love to strut their stuff; and (2) the West is devoid of anything even remotely resembling an ocean.

The year was 1961, and our steel-blue Thunderbird was pulling a sixteen-foot trailer through the high country around Glacier National Park in northern Montana.

Dad had never driven with a trailer in tow, which accounted for why he didn't give the growing winds a second thought as he wound his way up, down, and around mountain road after mountain road.

It was nearing noon, and I was resting my head comfortably between the front bucket seats when I overheard the Road Warrior exhorting the Navigator to "hold on." I knew something was wrong by the tone in Dad's voice. As Bill Cosby used to say, when an operating physician says "Oops," you know it's time to panic.

I bolted upright—just in time to see the reflection of our trailer in the rearview mirror. The trailer appeared to be floating above the car and waving back and forth like the tail on a dog. Dad hurriedly turned the steering wheel in a frantic attempt to regain control of the trailer, but in so doing snapped the hitch off the rear bumper, sending our trailer airborne.

Like my adventure along the seashore, the entire episode took only seconds. And as we came to a safe rest (God's grace) perpendicular to the stunned traffic stopped in either direction, we stared in disbelief at the trailer, which now rested precariously at the edge of a cliff.

Everything was in disarray. Clothes were strewn everywhere, mixed with exotic combinations of foodstuffs (broken syrup bottles, crushed cans of dripping meats, vegetables, fruits, and so forth) and household cleansers. Only a dozen eggs survived intact! Along with one thousand paper plates.

Indeed, it was these paper plates that provided some much-needed humor in an otherwise discouraging day. Because of their position in the trailer, and because of the direction of the winds hitting the wreckage, the plates were being picked up one at a time and sent flying—Frisbee-like—into the valley below.

"UFOS LAND IN MONTANA! RANCHERS COUNT HUNDREDS IN REAL-LIFE MARTIAN INVASION!"

Sorry to disappoint you, boys, it was just us Smiths.

Yes, humor and grace prepared me for anything the road could throw at me—even traveling an additional two weeks in that steel-blue Thunderbird with a trailer full of clothes, souvenirs, and a rack of deer horns in the backseat, an end of which seemed permanently lodged in my right nostril.

Still, our vacations were larger than life. Hardly restful, many times downright nail-biting, but in retrospect fun—strained bladders and impaired nostrils notwithstanding. Which is why I carry the vacation passion like a precious family heirloom. Yes, I have the travel bug bad. How bad? Well, let me put it this way. If you ever have trouble finding someone to show your two thousand vacation slides to, just give me a call.

And like my father before me, I am determined to pass this precious heirloom on to the next generation of Road Warriors—namely, my wife, Judy, and sons, Andrew and Kevin.

Which is the story of this book.

YOUR "PERFECT VACATION" PLANNER
Things to remember on the holiday road.

❖

Be forewarned: You will lose all sense of taste once you walk into your first souvenir shop. How else can you explain your fascination with that "authentic Western" wallclock made out of "authentic Western" buffalo chips?

Section One

❖

Do You, Judy, Take This Road Map?

2

"I Left My Lunch in San Francisco"

As they look ahead to married life, a man and his fiancée invariably ask each other a lot of questions. Questions that help would-be husbands and wives better understand each other. Questions that help them build a foundational framework upon which a marriage can grow.

"Should we live in an apartment or buy a house?"

"What kind of music do you like?"

"Do you want to have children?"

"Do you like anchovies on your pizza?"

Like all couples before us, Judy and I asked each other these and 101 other questions. We took time to answer each honestly, and with each answer we became more certain our marriage would not only stand the test of time, but would rank among the world's greatest unions.

We soon discovered, however, that we didn't ask all of the questions we should have asked. Such as the *one really important question* that somehow slipped my mind: "Do you like to travel?" and its critical corollaries: "Where do you like to go on vacation?" and "Would you drive thirty-six nonstop hours to

15

California in a tin can (our car was a sub-subcompact) and have the audacity to say you had fun?"

I can't believe I, of all people, overlooked these foundational questions. Imagine me marrying someone who didn't thrill to endless highways, scorching deserts, and snowy mountain tops in the dead of summer. Imagine me being committed for life to someone who didn't long to read a road map, or who didn't feel a thrill each time she crossed a state line!

"Welcome to Illinois, the Land of Lincoln." It's enough to make the pulse quicken and the imagination run wild!

So unimaginable was it for me to consider that such a person existed, I simply assumed that Judy was made of the same travel stuff I was. Moreover, I reasoned that Judy, having never been west of the Mississippi, was more eager than I to hit the back-forty blacktop and experience the "real" America.

Confident that my soon-to-be-bride would be ecstatic over wherever I chose for our first week together (such are the naive expectations of every newlywed), and knowing she was too busy with wedding plans to worry about the "where" of our honeymoon, I went ahead and took charge of the arrangements. Judy trusted me implicitly—and I would not disappoint.

It didn't take me long to settle on *the* ideal romantic getaway: California. Why California? It had mountains (my favorite vacation destination) and beaches (Judy's favorite destinations). It was a perfect compromise—and, after all, wasn't marriage supposed to be built on compromise?

We would travel by car. We could have seven thousand miles of just relating to one another, of learning what makes the other tick.

But wait. We only had a week's time. Thirty-six hours there and thirty-six back would leave us with only four days to experience the whole of California. Sure, we would have plenty of time to talk, but California would be only a blur.

What to do? The adventurer within me said go for it. But then again, here was a golden opportunity to model a "better way" and consider the other person. To put her welfare before my own.

I reasoned that while the purpose of a honeymoon is physical closeness, seven thousand miles in a front seat designed to comfortably handle half a person might be a little too much togetherness for the first week of married life. So in a moment of surprising restraint and maturity, I opted to have my bride and me suffer cramped discomfort for only three-and-a-half hours aboard economy seats on American flight 123.

A week before the big day, I picked up our tickets, made rental car and hotel reservations, and told Judy of our honeymoon dream. She politely smiled, then told me I needed to make sure my groomsmen made it to the rehearsal on time.

I was right. She was thrilled!

The best I can figure it, honeymoons were designed to help new husbands and wives confront their differences immediately—a heavy trip when all you really want to do is enjoy the girl of your dreams on the world's most extended—and costly—date. Oh, sure there's the sex thing. (Which, as Judy and I eventually discovered, was worth the wait.) But what premarital counseling doesn't tell you is that twenty-four-hour-a-day nonstop togetherness for the first seven consecutive days of married life is akin to stepping on an exposed 220 wire. It's a shock.

On that first evening, however, Judy and I were so tired we barely noticed the initial jolts. Sure she gagged herself while brushing her teeth; and okay, I sang Italian in the shower, but these were hardly irreconcilable differences.

These would come later.

The next morning we landed in Los Angeles exhausted, but as the designated travel cheerleader, I sprang immediately into action. We would first visit Disneyland, then explore Hearst Castle along the breathtaking California coast highway, and finally eat Chinese food in San Francisco. And all along the way we would leisurely stop along the shoreline, breathe in the ocean,

"HOW WAS I SUPPOSED TO KNOW WE WERE SETTING THE TENT UP IN A DRIED CREEK BED?!"

and look longingly, lovingly into each other's eyes.

It sounded good on paper. But as I should have known—and as Judy would soon learn—the best-made Smith plans have a way of colliding headlong into reality.

For starters, our honeymoon happened to coincide with the first official United States gas crisis. In the L.A. area, the crisis was at its height. Gas was being rationed, stations were open only on select days, and gas lines approached a half-mile in length. All this made waiting for your precious ten gallons of gas similar to waiting in line at Disneyland to ride "Pirates of the Caribbean." The only difference was Disney tickets were cheaper!

We not only had to keep careful measure of our fuel consumption, but also take advantage of any public restrooms that happened to be open—whether we needed relief or not. As I recall, Wednesday was a particularly painful day, with almost every gas station (and consequently every restroom) closed. We therefore limited our coffee consumption on that day to half a cup each—and saved the cup, just in case.

Fortunately, our rental car was a Ford Pinto. Not the safest of vehicles mind you, what with growing accusations that its gas tank was a tinderbox ready to blow. But its gas mileage was extraordinary by the standards of the day—over twenty miles to the gallon. Meaning, we could confidently make the run from L.A. to San Francisco on a single fill-up.

It didn't mean, however, that Judy would have the confidence to take her eyes off the gas gauge.

One of the many discoveries I uncovered in the course of the week was that Judy is not a worrier. She's one of the most unflappable woman I've ever known—except when it comes to tripping along some unfamiliar holiday road. Then, control over this foreign environment becomes her first priority:

Do we know where we're going?

Have we made room reservations for tonight?

Do we have enough gas to get there?

And, as Judy would discover in the course of the week, I *am* a worrier. Except when it comes to traveling those same never-before-traveled roads. Then the adventure and challenge of overcoming a new environment plays to my machismo: you know, man against nature, man against man, man against rising gas prices.

Do I know where we're going? Why should I? Let's have fun and play our destination by ear.

Reservations? Don't worry. There are plenty of places to stay where we're going.

Enough gas? You gotta be kidding. We could drive from L.A. to New York and back again! And still do this coastline drive.

The California coastline may well be the most scenic—and sobering—drive in the continental United States.

What begins as a fairly flat drive from L.A. to San Luis Obispo (site of the Hearst Castle) suddenly turns into a winding, desolate incline with your vehicle rarely farther than three or four feet from an edge that plummets hundreds of feet into the Pacific Ocean below. Adding to the driving challenge is the condition of the road itself. I assume little has been done to this highway since the days of the horse and buggy. While the wagon ruts are gone, they've been replaced by potholes and crevices, some of which you swear could eat a Pinto for lunch.

And as if all this didn't present enough of a challenge, there are no places to stop for gas. Or food. Or lodging. Or, for that matter, anything else. It's just you and the highway. You and that ever deepening drop-off just to your left. . . . You and your wife.

"So Harold, you're sure we have enough gas to get to Monterey?"

"Yes, dear. Remember? We filled up yesterday. And besides, it's Wednesday. There are no stations open today anyway."

"Oh, great!"

"Judy," I said in my most reassuring voice, "don't worry. Everything's fine. I love you."

"I love you, too," replied Judy, "which is why it bums me out to think we'll probably be found dead here. I can see the front page now: 'GAS SHORTAGE CLAIMS TWO LIVES ALONG DESOLATE STRETCH OF COASTAL HIGHWAY.' "

We were only three days into marital bliss and I was sensing yet another difference between me and my beautiful and nervous bride. Gagging over toothbrushes was one thing, but not losing oneself in the travel experience was something else completely. My plans for future eventful family vacations were being threatened. The Smith travel legacy was at stake.

So, I determined to win my woman over to the wonders of travel by redirecting our deteriorating conversation to the majestic scenery all around us. The mountains. The ocean. And the canyon that seemed to come out of nowhere, which we were heading straight toward.

"Oh, look at that canyon, Jude! Isn't it beautiful!"

"Harold!" screamed Judy.

Her scream was well-timed. Another couple of seconds, and the two of us would have floated majestically over the canyon ridge and into the ocean below.

"I'll concentrate on the scenery," scolded Judy. "You concentrate on keeping us on the road."

I thought it best after that to let my new wife simply take in God's creation on her own. Like a dutiful husband, I contented myself with only glimpses to my right and left. After all, what good would all my future family vacation plans be if we were dead?

By nightfall, we reached Monterey. And happily for me and my diminishing reputation, with plenty of gas to spare.

The fact that we survived the coastline drive, and didn't reach Monterey merely on fumes, seemed to be a travel turning point in our now four-day-old marriage. With the exception of our near canyon free-fall, I had proven to Judy that her Road Warrior could be trusted with both the gas tank and her life. Judy admitted that the preceding day's drive was indeed one of the most majestic she had ever experienced. Perhaps the most majestic.

All of this was music to my ears. Judy was taking her first steps toward becoming a Smith! And she now seemed determined to take a quantum leap once we arrived in San Francisco. She wanted to really experience Chinatown. Listen to its languages. Breathe in its atmosphere. Feast on its foods.

We began day five of our honeymoon by walking through the enormous entrance arch of Chinatown and meandering from shop to shop to shop. By noon, our cross-cultural adventure had left us starving, so it was off to the nearest restaurant for the ultimate culinary experience.

I wish I knew exactly what we ate. It was the day's special and, as best I recall, it was round, somewhat translucent, and soft on the inside. Judy went at it with the same relish I had attacked the California coastline. Yes, the Smiths were on vacation and the newest Smith was now beginning to partake of the family's legacy for adventure.

Unfortunately, she partook of too much legacy. Within minutes of me paying the bill, Judy started feeling the day's special doing *tae kwon do* in her stomach. Wisdom dictated we put an abrupt end to the day's adventures and high-tail it back to our hotel. Which we did. But not before stopping at the seventeen public restrooms between the restaurant and our parked car.

The Smith vacation legacy had hit full force!

Only by the evening of day six—the last evening of our honeymoon—was Judy able to sit up and take nourishment.

However, seeing our dream trip drawing quickly to a close, I dared to ask her if she was well enough to make one last foray into the city, this time to Fisherman's Wharf. She said she was. (What a woman!) And that night we experienced the flavors of France at a little cafe overlooking San Francisco Bay.

In between trips to the bathroom, Judy assured me she'd do it all over again. We were indeed beginning to overcome our differences and forge a relationship.

I had found a travel partner for life!

YOUR "PERFECT VACATION" PLANNER
Things to remember on the holiday road.

Just remember what mother told you: The only essential change of clothing to take on your vacation is lots of clean underwear.

3

"Dear Mother Nature"

In chapter 1 I mentioned the name of Clark Griswold, National Lampoon's vacation "iron man." While a world-class buffoon, Clark nevertheless represented all us travelholics who see family travel as an almost transcendental experience linking soul to nature and soul to soul.

Trouble is, my wife is not of the Griswold lineage. Judy prefers lying on some secluded beach with a good book to driving eight hundred miles every day for two weeks. Yet back in 1975 when our marriage was but a year old, she gladly (bravely?) agreed to what I assured her would be the adventure of a lifetime—our first major "family vacation" as man and wife. Our destination was Yellowstone National Park, and along the way we would not only find America (specifically, the Badlands, Mount Rushmore, the Grand Tetons, and the Rockies), but we would discover each other. And we would do it all in just two weeks!

After all, we're the Smiths, and we can do anything!

The first day found us traveling across southern Michigan and northern Illinois—which, translated, means a pretty boring drive. To break the monotony we did the usual stuff—counted rest areas, sang the Top Ten, played an assortment of license plate games and talked. Oh, how we talked—and usually about all the fun we were going to have.

On day two, the air-conditioning cut out in Iowa and the talking drew to an abrupt halt in the 100-degree heat. Complicating matters was an "environmental warning" cautioning people against driving with windows open and allowing polluted air into their cars! But not to worry. We were discovering each other! For one thing, neither of us had ever seen the other sweat so much.

By the third day, our bodies had become one with the vinyl seat covers. But hey, we were exploring *our* country! Not even a tornado in Loveland, Colorado—to which we were uneasy eye-witnesses—dimmed our enthusiasm. Well, *my* enthusiasm.

By the time we got to Jackson, Wyoming, the temperature had started to drop, and we looked forward to spending three invigorating days in this majestic heart of the Grand Teton Mountain Range. The highlight would be a leisurely, five-hour journey down the Snake River in a twelve-person raft.

As we reached the halfway point of this once-in-a-lifetime white-water excursion, ominous cloud formations appeared over the mountain peaks. And out of the clouds forked lightning bolts—pointed straight at us. Our guide summarized our predicament: "Ladies and gentlemen, we have a world-class electrical storm heading our way—and we're on water." His nervous chuckle left no question that this was bad.

Then came the clincher: "Unfortunately, portage is two-and-a-half hours in either direction, so the only thing we can do is press onward and try to outrun the storm."

At that moment I made eye contact with my beautiful wife. I didn't so much read fear in her eyes as I read, "Harold, next year we're taking books to the beach."

By the time we got to Yellowstone, the temperature had bottomed out somewhere in the thirties, snow was on the ground, and we were forced to buy warm clothing—at the usual inflated park prices. Nevertheless, the majestic mountainsides, the deep canyons and, of course, the assorted geysers and mud pots quickly made us forget the "challenges" of the first part of the trip.

Until our last day in the park.

As any Griswold—or Smith—will tell you, part of the joy of vacationing is learning beforehand all there is to know about your destination. I had read a great deal about the history of this, America's first national park, and was pontificating about an earthquake that had reshaped certain park landscapes when Judy pointed out an unusual roadblock about one hundred feet ahead of us. It was a boulder the size of a three-bedroom bungalow.

"Wow," I said rather boyishly. "Must be a strong wind." (Remember, Clark Griswold wasn't exactly quick on the draw.)

When we finally stopped for lunch, we found park rangers scurrying hither and yon. The word *earthquake* rumbled through the cafeteria.

"Winds?" Judy sarcastically asked. "Right."

Because the quake—6.5 on the Richter scale—had knocked out portions of two or three main roads, it took us hours to get back to the Old Faithful Lodge. Once there, we eagerly packed our bags (we were to leave the next morning) and readied ourselves for bed.

With pillows propped, we finally relaxed—Judy with her book and me with my *Time* magazine. Then the bed started shaking.

"Hey, babe," I said. "Whaddaya doing? I'm trying to read." Engrossed in some subplot, Judy didn't respond. But no matter. The bed was now still. I returned to the week's events.

One or two minutes passed, then the bed started swaying again.

"Hon," I said, "stop rocking the bed."

"Harold, I'm not rocking the bed."

I expected a grinning Rod Serling to walk into our undulating room and welcome my wife and me to "The Twilight Zone."

But then, Rod probably wasn't dumb enough to vacation with a Griswold. I sprang to my feet, only to stumble back into the bed as the entire room rocked from side to side.

"More wind?" Judy asked.

Two aftershocks were enough for this Midwesterner. We got our clothes on and slept in the car. The thought of a fast getaway made our subcompact seem safer than a one hundred-year-old wood structure.

The next morning, bleary-eyed, we headed for home, which we reached in four days. (Actually, we could have made it in three if our car hadn't died on I-94 in Michigan—on the Fourth of July.) Along the way, Judy volunteered to play the part of a Griswold and offer her own vacation suggestions for the next six decades:

Jamaica.

Miami.

St. Thomas.

Bermuda.

Honolulu.

Always a quick study—I got the picture.

The ensuing years found us vacationing at various beaches. But once a Griswold, always a Griswold. Fifteen years later (see chapter 17), I won Judy's blessing to embark on yet another Yellowstone adventure. Her rationale: It would be good for our sons. (Plus too much sun can be hazardous to your health.)

Andrew and Kevin had yet to experience the wonders of the American West—not to mention the joys of cross-country, interstate-highway travel. I was confident that once they saw their first wild chipmunk, they'd be hooked for life—and the Smith family vacation legacy would continue unabated into the next generation.

But just to hedge my bets, I checked my AAA TripTik to see if there were any good beaches in Wyoming.

Adapted from the article, "The Iron Man Takes a Vacation," *Marriage Partnership*, Summer 1990.

YOUR "PERFECT VACATION" PLANNER
Things to remember on the holiday road.

❖

The emergency roadside telephone you desperately need will be temporarily out of order.

4

All This for a Beach Vacation?

CLEARWATER BEACH, FLORIDA, 1989
It's ironic that Judy's favorite vacation spots all include "beach" in the title, when you figure her number-one phobia concerns a very basic sand-and-surf necessity.

The bathing suit.

No, Judy wasn't frightened by a size twenty bikini when she was prepubescent. Rather, it's shopping for this particular beach accouterment that sends her into shock—and more often than not, sends her annually into the local grocery store for a summer's supply of Strawberry Ultra Slim-Fast, the drink that replaces Diet Coke as Judy's recurrent beverage of choice.

Actually, Judy hates Strawberry Ultra Slim-Fast. It tastes like flavored chalk dust and, if improperly blended, leaves an inch of grit on your back teeth.

But this momentary agony is nothing compared to the true grit Judy says it takes to wear a bathing suit in public—even if the beach or pool is a million miles from home. According to my wife, she has enough flaws in her fabric to avoid wearing anything revealing until the year 2051—at which time she'll be around one hundred and much too old for designer swimwear.

For the life of me, I can't figure where this woman, with eyes that could make any *Glamour* girl blink with envy, learned to equate bathing suits with certain medieval forms of torture. (Of course, she would argue that you could at least hide in an iron maiden.) I have never experienced such trauma and remain happy to wear the same suit I wore when we visited our first beach together, oh, about twenty-five pounds ago. Such body confidence comfortably "fits" a Road Warrior—even if his suit doesn't!

But I digress.

I experienced Judy's body panic firsthand when we went shopping for a new bathing suit for her to wear in anticipation of our visiting Clearwater Beach in Florida.

"Well, Hon, what do you think?" my wife-turned-fitting-room-model asked warily.

"I think you look beautiful, Sweetie. It's you!"

"I don't look like Tubby the Tuba, do I?"

"Of course not. Go ahead. Get it."

"You don't think I'll look out-of-place on the beach with all those svelte blondes in their thong suits?"

"What's a thong suit?"

"Very funny."

"No, seriously, if it makes you feel any better, we could vacation at a dude ranch and wear bulky flannel shirts and leather chaps. They don't make thong chaps do they?"

"Oh, Harold. I want to go to the beach. I love the water."

"So why don't you spend more time in the water? If worse comes to worse," I said jokingly, "you could always hide in it."

"Ha, ha. I don't go into the water because I don't want to ruin my hair."

"So let me get this straight. You love beach vacations, but you hate buying and wearing a bathing suit, and you hate swimming because the wet head is dead."

"Right. You don't think it's too tight, do you?" she asked, poking and prodding at her waist, hips, chest, shoulders.

"You look great! Hey, maybe we could take some time off and just watch travel videos for a week. You know, pull the shades, turn off the lights, and travel to the uttermost parts of the world—and be seen by no one!"

"I need to lose ten pounds."

"For the last time, Judy, you look great. I could eat you up. I can't wait to show you off to all the people on Clearwater Beach we don't know. Go ahead, buy it."

"Well, I'll think about it."

Translation: "I'm fat."

Back the accursed garment goes, to be replaced by other kinder, gentler, off-the-rack fashions. About 104 of them in total.

Sometime during that long, long evening, a suit was finally purchased, but not without Judy's self-imposed stipulation to lose ten pounds before she'd wear it or before she found matching sandals (or whichever came first).

I went home exhausted. All this, I thought, for a beach vacation!

Now don't get me wrong. I wouldn't want Judy buying anything that makes her feel uncomfortable. It's just that the way she sees herself and the way I see her are two different ways of seeing. And so as the "Countdown to Clearwater" continued, it fell to me to convince her that she needn't hide herself under a beach umbrella or bury her body in the Gulf-side sand.

Which brings me back to Strawberry Ultra Slim-Fast. Four weeks before heading south, Judy triumphantly announced at dinner one night that a precious few pounds had been shed. I applauded her willpower. But hearing the announcement, our two sons (then ages ten and seven) seemed only mildly impressed. Said Andrew, our oldest: "You're already the most beautiful lady in the world."

Out of the mouths of babes.

Judy, happily, took Andrew's heartfelt compliment at face

value and was genuinely encouraged—to the point where she even suggested she might be willing to throw self-confidence to the wind and set a foot in the Atlantic.

That's not to say we completely transformed Judy's view of swimwear. I figure she'll never enjoy wearing a bathing suit or shopping for one—despite her love of beaches. But at the same time, maybe that night's dinner conversation helped her see she doesn't have to compete with some toothy clone in *Glamour* for our attention. Or some lithesome thong on Clearwater Beach. We like her just the way she is and we try to tell her that every single day—even when she's not fussing over a suit.

So Clearwater Beach was a success. We swam (all of us!), tanned, then swam some more. Judy was the foxiest woman on the beach—the few thong suits notwithstanding. And a good time was had by all.

But next year, I'm suggesting we vacation out West. After all, mountain clothing is looser fitting and chaps are definitely an emotionally easier buy!

Adapted from Harold B. Smith, "My Day in Swimwear," *A Scruffy Husband Is a Happy Husband* (Colorado Springs: Focus on the Family, 1992).

❖

The car trouble you experience while circumnavigating some backwater hamlet will undoubtedly be "the most dadblasted thing" the local mechanic has ever seen.

5

Next Time, We Drive to Hawaii!

The term "Road Warrior" implies an affinity to that basic mode of twentieth-century transportation—the automobile. So not surprisingly, this "RW" will invariably choose four wheels planted securely on terra firma to anything suspended in the air or adrift on the sea. Oh, sure, a plane is faster. And yes, you can eat more on a Carnival cruise. But travel by car *is* safer—if only because you're in control.

And control is everything to a Road Warrior. Which is why the thought of flying over the Pacific to get to Hawaii was a sobering thought indeed.

However, while spending endless hours airborne over the world's largest ocean is definitely not my idea of a good time (Amelia Aerhart's sentiments exactly), it's downright invigorating to Judy. She loves planes and is always encouraging her earthbound husband with myriad statistics showing airplanes as the safest way to travel.

On rare occasions I have capitulated to her sales pitches and boldly gone where few in their right minds would ever want to go— six miles skyward in economy class. (The condensed seating alone

35

is enough to make you swear off flying!) Throughout each of these infrequent airborne excursions, I hold on to Judy's hand like a drowning swimmer clings to a life ring. Yes, I may be a Road Warrior, but there are times I depend on Judy's strength and confidence.

Of course, when your destination is way over there, then air travel is probably your only travel choice. Which means you are stuck with one of two options: You can either content yourself with seeing only what you can get to by car, or you can get on a plane and pray your life insurance premiums are all paid up. The fact that our Hawaii-bound flight was taking off from South Korea's Kempo Airport obviously tells you which of these options I chose—albeit reluctantly.

As we boarded our Korean Air 747 and took our bulkhead seats (with an emergency exit immediately to our left), I did what I always do when I first board a plane: I prayed. Then I looked for structural damage. Does the overhead compartment close? Does the seat recline? Can I ring for a flight attendant? These may seem inconsequential, but I figure if the answer to any of these is "no," then who's to say the wing or engine won't just drop off in mid-flight?

With my safety inspection complete and everything appearing functional, I contented myself with a magazine and waited for takeoff. Judy was already deep into her own book, secure in the knowledge that her husband had everything under control. Estimated flight time was eight hours, and dinner would be served shortly after reaching our cruising altitude.

A storm was moving into the area, and strong winds began buffeting the plane as it taxied down the runway and then lifted into the air. It was an older model 747, designed shortly after Kitty Hawk. And steadily increasing turbulence shook every loose-fitting joint in its antiquated, economy-class cabin, creating an in-flight cacophony of bangs, pops, and squeaks.

My discomfort level grew with each wind sheer, although I thought that once we reached cruising altitude, the constant shaking would cease.

I was wrong. At thirty-five thousand feet, the plane shook more violently than ever.

I was feeling out of control.

"We're gonna die," I mumbled to Judy.

"Oh, Harold, no we're not. It's just a little wind." But no sooner had she said that then the plane dropped about one thousand feet, leaving dinner trays on laps, on the floor, and even on the ceiling!

"Okay," Judy conceded. "It's not a little wind."

It was going to be a long flight.

Still, I hadn't given up hope. Judy didn't seem overly concerned that our lives were about to be snuffed out before their prime. Nor, for that matter, did our pilot.

If a Road Warrior can't be in control of a situation, then he wants the assurance that someone else he can trust *is* in control. And when you're shaking along the friendly skies, that someone can only be the pilot. But for some reason, our pilot wasn't talking. Maybe he was preoccupied with the thought of ditching his craft in the ocean below. Whatever the reason, his lack of communication with the passengers made our roller-coaster ride all the more nerve-racking.

And the lack of clear communication between flight attendants and passengers didn't help much either. From what I could tell, the only English our two cabin attendants spoke was "yes" and "Coke."

"Excuse me," I asked our flight attendant. "Are we going to die?"

No response. Just a blank stare. Followed by one of those unconvincing smiles with accompanying multiple nods.

"Excuse me," I said again. "Are we going into the drink?"

"Ah," said the flight attendant, nodding even more furiously. "Yes. Coke."

Very comforting.

Finally, after watching the "Fasten Seat Belt" warning light burn brightly for three solid hours, we heard the captain's barely audible voice come over the crackling intercom.

"Ladies and gentleman," our pilot said in his heavy Korean accent, "yes" and "Coke." Or something to that effect.

I was convinced we were done for. My only consolation was knowing that when we did go down, there would be plenty of Coke for everyone. I looked over at Judy—my last source of hope. She, too, was beginning to show signs of panic. Her breathing was noticeably more labored. My own feelings of doom intensified.

Why did we choose Hawaii? I thought. *Why did we choose Korean Air?*

And why in heaven's name had we not chosen someplace we could drive to?

By the halfway mark, our flight cabin looked like my sons' bedrooms. Overhead luggage racks had dumped their cargo all along the aisle. Dinner debris was everywhere. And air sickness bags were full to overflowing. Literally. And still the plane tossed to and fro.

Judy and I were now clinging to each other, as if we could somehow stabilize our row of seats.

"Still like flying?" I asked Judy.

"Very funny," she replied, this time keeping her copious knowledge of air flight safety statistics to herself.

Suddenly, another major drop in elevation occurred, prompting more screams and more requests for assistance. This time, however, our brave attendants—I assume on captain's orders—ignored the hundred or so "request lights" igniting their work station, and high-tailed it down the luggage-strewn aisle. They dropped themselves into the two seats directly facing Judy and me on the other side of the bulkhead. They quickly buckled themselves in place, smiled a contemplative smile, then bowed toward us.

"This is it!" I cried to Judy.

But instead, it was more of the same. In fact, two more hours of more of the same. Until dawn, when I could look through our passenger window and see we were finally moving out of a major tropical storm and into Pacific blue calm. The flight attendants who had now been across from us for the last two hours casually unbuckled their safety belts and prepared to deal with all the passengers in need. Beginning with us.

"Coke?" asked one of them, no doubt noticing the ashen looks on our faces.

To which we both answered: "Yes."

❖

*The extra charge for a
poolside room is hardly worth it.
Unless, of course, you want to
pay to be kept awake by
forty-seven unattended children
who have to scream
and dive into the pool
"just one more time."*

6

Adventures in
Undersea Camping

If you ever have the "opportunity" to drive through Kearney, Nebraska, then by all means stop by Cabela's Sporting Goods. The size of your average urban mall, the big "C" rightly boasts every piece of camping, hunting, and fishing equipment ever conceived. And more.

You say you want a fly caster with a removable turbolure? No problem.

A pearl-handled, single-shot, carbine with copper-coated twin sights? Right over there.

Triple-insulated rubber hikers with the patented double-strength ewe ties? You bet! In both men's and women's sizes!

Perhaps most impressive is Cabela's exhaustive array of camping equipment attractively presented in "lifelike" frescoes: one-, two-, ten-man tents, lamps, stoves, toasters, a zillion-and-one dehydrated foodstuffs, water purifiers, convection ovens, microwaves (microwaves?)—literally everything a man, woman, and child could possibly need to make their wilderness adventure more like a night at the Hilton with a guaranteed view.

For outdoorsmen and wannabes alike, Cabela's tempts you

to test your mettle against all the great outdoors can throw at you. It lulls you into thinking you *can* take on the great outdoors and win!

Of course, I'm not taken in by any of it. Neither is my wife. We know those happy Cabela's mannequins eating rubber pheasant by a roaring red-plastic fire in front of their water-resistant, made-in-America, family-sized tent have never camped with the Smiths.

If they had, their plastic smiles would have long since melted.

Actually, camping is okay if your idea of fun is not sleeping, not washing, and not eating anything even remotely recognizable. I learned this in 1973 when I bicycled—with about twenty-five other teens and young adults—around New England for two weeks.

Beginning in Albany, New York, we intended to ride through New York, Massachusetts, New Hampshire, and Maine, and commune with nature each night in some breathtaking campsite. The problem was we never reached camp before nightfall—which meant assembling thirteen impossible canvas tents by the light of either a fire (which itself took four hours to start!) or by six or seven dying flashlights. None of us ever got to bed before two in the morning.

Cooking in near total blackness was another equally frustrating experience, and usually meant resigning oneself to a dinner of granola bars (if you could find them), maybe a melted Three Musketeers bar from your back pocket, and water. Warm Coke was optional.

By day three, all this communing with nature was getting to me. I hadn't had this much fun since the last time I had food poisoning (which was on day two). The better part of valor dictated I get out before my health and sanity were threatened.

Unfortunately, I failed to listen to my own common sense, and somewhere north of Lexington, Massachusetts, the rains came—and they stayed for the rest of our trip.

Cycling in a diluvial downpour is bad enough. But going through the painful process of setting up camp, cooking dinner, breaking down camp—and doing it all in a monsoon—is downright Sisyphusian in nature. A water-logged version of hell. The final straw came the evening of day seven when my soggy sleeping bag, supported on an air mattress, started floating toward the tent opening. With me in it.

My dislike of camping is equaled only by Judy's aversion to sleeping under the stars. And while the genesis of her bias is less dramatic than mine, it is by no means less determined. She has this thing about running water and privacy—two commodities not always available when you're communing with nature. Judy's motto: If it has to be camping, it has to be Camp Hilton.

Truly, we are one flesh when it comes to this form of recreational torture. And we can both rest in the fact that one of us won't force the other into a sleeping bag, or have him or her eat an evening meal cooked and charred over an open fire. That is, unless the destination is Walt Disney World in Orlando, Florida.

Before 1979 I had not had the privilege of experiencing the Magic Kingdom. So when my sister invited me and Judy to join her family and Dad and Mom (Road Warrior and Navigator) at Disney's Fort Wilderness Park, how could I say no?

"There's plenty of running water, Jude," I tried to say convincingly. "And my sister assures me there are clean bathrooms aplenty."

"And privacy?"

"Plenty of that, too. Private showers. Private stalls. Heck, more privacy than you have here! Besides," I continued, "it's Disney. How bad can it be?"

"I don't know," she answered skeptically. "But I'm sure we'll find out."

Spoken like a true Smith!

The skies were only beginning to darken when we arrived at our campsite ("Quail Trail") late on a Sunday afternoon. Our home

DESPERATE PEOPLE DO DESPERATE THINGS,
AND THE HILLMANS WERE VERY
DESPERATE PEOPLE.

for the next five days, which would also house my sister and her husband, Jim, was already pitched. My folks' sixteen-foot trailer was parked next door.

Smiles were abundant that evening as we fixed a camp dinner that was actually edible and talked about the great time we would all have in the Magic Kingdom. We played cards by Coleman lantern and, between hands, listened to the singing of birds and the chirping of insects in the woods all around us. *How peaceful,* I thought. Perhaps the Cabela's mannequins were right.

By 10:00 o'clock it was time for bed. We had a big day—a big week—ahead of us, and a good night's sleep would help us all get off on the right foot. The four of us went off to our sleeping bags while Mom, Dad, and their two young nieces headed for the trailer.

Surrounded by the stillness of Floridian darkness and nestled cozily in our sleeping bags, I kissed Judy goodnight and whispered that our first day camping as husband and wife had been a complete success.

"Perhaps we're wrong," I said. "Maybe camping *is* the way to travel."

"Let's wait and see," Judy replied.

And with that, we drifted off to dreamland.

I can't recall if it was the thunderclap or the lightning bolt just outside our tent that awakened the four of us from our reverie. Whatever it was, it was followed by a downpour that quickly turned the twenty feet between our tent and the trailer into a tropical quagmire. It was a foretaste of worse to come.

"It looks like they've moved the jungle cruise to Fort Wilderness," I said, hoping a little levity would lift our long faces—Judy's being the longest.

Nobody was amused.

"Not to worry though," I continued, "we can all stay dry in the trailer and wait out the storm."

One by one we slogged off to the trailer. And waited. Two, three, four hours, and still the storm raged on. By early afternoon, our collective moods started feeling the strain. Er, rain.

"C'mon kids," encouraged Dad, always the optimist. "We're not gonna let a little rain [now about four inches] keep us from having fun, are we?"

It was a difficult question for Judy and me to answer. Visions of permanently wrinkled skin filled our minds. But so too did the much anticipated fun and frolic of the Magic Kingdom. "No," we unconvincingly answered the Road Warrior. "This rain will not ruin our fun." And with halfhearted sighs, we grabbed umbrellas and waded to Cinderella's Castle.

"Maybe camping *is* the way to travel," whispered Judy sarcastically, recalling my harebrained observation from the night before and eying the mud now halfway up her shoes.

I could only smile and assure her things would get better. But, of course, she knew better.

By midweek, over twenty inches of precipitation had fallen on sections of central Florida, and Disney World had a new exhibit—the Fort Wilderness Rain Forest—featuring the species Smith as part of the primordial soup. Among the highlights:

- ◆ permanently wet hair that defied even mousse;
- ◆ permanently wet clothing that had shrunk an average of two sizes;
- ◆ and permanently wet sleeping bags that gave the term "waterbed" new meaning.

The only thing not dampened was our enjoyment of each other. We laughed about the record rains, we laughed about our dashed hopes (like getting a tan!), and we laughed that yet another family vacation had fallen victim to THE SURPRISE FACTOR.

"We're the Smiths, and everything happens to us!"

As we squeegeed into our sleeping bags for the last time, we resigned ourselves to the incessant staccato of rain and the drip,

drip, drip of water leaking through six—make that seven—locations around the tent. Sleep nevertheless came quickly, but was periodically interrupted by a vengeful drip on our colliding air mattresses—now floating on two inches of water.

"Okay, so maybe camping *isn't* the way to travel," I whispered into my wife's wet ear. "But we have plenty of running water."

❖

While Judy and I have occasional disagreements about where to go on vacation and what to do, we have never—at least not since Fort Wilderness—had any disagreement about camping. Sure, we still are impressed with the Cabela's wilderness wish list, and we even bought one of those nifty, easy-to-assemble dome tents for backyard overnighters. But never again will we willingly expose ourselves to the great outdoors—unless there's a private room and private shower waiting for us at the end of the day.

We may be Smiths. But we're not stupid.

YOUR "PERFECT VACATION" PLANNER
Things to remember on the holiday road.

❖

The nearest rest stop is

always too far away.

The nearest clean rest stop

is nonexistent.

7

A Good Night's Rest Is Hard to Find

LONDON, ENGLAND, 1993

Not only do Judy and I see eye to eye on camping, but we also boast "high" standards when it comes to a night's lodging: I need a bed, Judy needs a clean bed and running water. And as a rule, we both get what we want—and usually a whole lot more. A case in point was the Osaka Hilton, or heaven to someone on a Smith budget.

We had been traveling for twenty-eight hours nonstop, venturing eastward from Chicago to Los Angeles to Anchorage to Seoul, and finally Osaka, in the south of Japan. Our ankles were swollen from all the sitting, and our clothing had an assortment of smells compliments of our 747 cattle car. I sat next to a fellow who I'm sure was a sumo wrestler returning to his homeland. For ten thousand miles he exhaled, I inhaled.

When we finally arrived at the Osaka Hilton, we were told by our travel reps that our luggage had been delayed, and that we would have at least two, maybe three hours to wait before we could change our clothes. This, on top of our jet lag, new breathing patterns, and two full days without sleep, sent us to our room as really ugly Americans. But once there, our temperaments quickly changed as we discovered the true meaning of five-star lodging. In the bathroom were all the toiletries a man and woman would ever want, let alone need. (We didn't use them all. Some, like the shower cap with Japanese calligraphy, made wonderful gifts.) In the closets were beautifully decorated oriental robes and cotton slippers. We could hit the showers with a vengeance, and not worry about being caught naked by the bellman bringing up our luggage.

Afterward, as we lounged, feet propped up, in our robes and slippers, we couldn't help but wonder what the poor people—or those not on a business travel account—were doing.

What "they" were probably doing was trying to find clean towels at a hostelry like the National, a roach motel somewhere in prehistoric Georgia. Actually, the National was not a place I visited with Judy (she'd have slept in the car if we had), but one that the original Road Warrior selected for his weary family as we made our way to Florida back in the early sixties.

A true Road Warrior, Dad drove until sunset and, if the kids weren't too restless or hungry, he then put in another two or three hours before calling it a day. Of course, the possible penalty for driving until 9:00 or 10:00 p.m. was not being able to find a place to spend the night. Or should I say, a *clean* place to spend the night.

Surprisingly, however, Dad's batting average for locating vacancies that at least had board of health approval was extraordinarily high. This was probably because when he stopped at a motel, he would ask the manager to escort him to the room in question so he could give it the once over. I never quite knew what exactly Dad was looking for—I assumed cleanliness. But then, if he was anything then like I am now, he was probably checking to see if the beds were comfortable—and if they had "Magic Fingers" for twenty-five cents.

If the room didn't meet with Dad's approval (say, the "Magic

Fingers" were broken), he'd move on to the next vacancy sign. As a rule, we found a "home" after only one or two inspections.

The National, however, was one world-class exception to this rule.

It was late. Later than usual, as I remember. And Road Warrior or no Road Warrior, the family had had enough. Eight hundred miles in one day was more than the rest of us mere mortals could handle, especially in one hundred-degree weather in a car that, of course, had no air conditioning.

Dad, sensing the emotional strain of his family—not to mention the mutinous look on the Navigator's face—began searching the countryside for a vacancy sign. But the harsh reality was there weren't any to be found. By 10:30 or 11:00, the possibility that we would be spending the night in our sweltering four-door was becoming more and more an almost certain reality.

Then, in the distance, a neon sign flickered, sputtering the word "Vacancy." A cheer went through the car.

As Dad pulled into the motel's parking lot, it was clear that this establishment would never appear on a "Deep South Segment" of *Lifestyles of the Rich and Famous*. Indeed, from where we sat, the question of structural integrity came to mind.

Nevertheless, it was late. With a motivational speech from the Navigator—"Honey, we take the room whatever it looks like, or else!"—Dad quickly disappeared behind the manager's door.

Only a minute or two passed before the Road Warrior reappeared victorious, jingling a set of keys in his hands for all of us to see. We had a room!

But a room that had more paint chips on the floor than paint on the ceiling. A room with a soap dish filled with scum so thick that slicing through it could have revealed the archeological find of the century. Of the millennium.

This place was bad. So bad, not even roaches would spend the night. It was so bad, we slept with our shoes on. After all, none of us wanted to risk infection by touching the floor with our bare feet.

Dad was embarrassed that his family had to be exposed to this breeding ground of diseases past and present. But he was livid that the "Magic Fingers" were out of order! His—and our—only resort was to sleep—and sleep in beds that literally sagged two feet in the middle of their mattresses. However, we were tired, and sleep—mercifully—came quickly.

The next morning, we decided not to shower (who knew what new and exciting life forms would be shot out of the spigot). Instead, we got dressed and left as quickly as possible—actually looking forward to another eight hundred miles in the car.

But we had made a memory. Even today, the word "National" remains a warning to any Smith who dares take potluck when it comes to a good night's lodging.

I remembered "National" vividly when my family and I arrived in London for two weeks in the British Isles recently. Lodging is exorbitant in the capital city (around $200 a night—without a bath), and the only hope for financial survival are the bed and breakfasts, which are proliferate throughout London and the rest of the U.K. The problem, however, is that many of these B&Bs are "National" in their presentation.

Like the one we spent two nights at in the Kensington High Street District.

The owner and host of this two hundred-year-old home was eastern European, I think Hungarian, and had a particularly brusque way about her. She always appeared to be preoccupied (maybe with her Hungarian-to-English dictionary), and would only intermittently acknowledge my presence. Making matters even more challenging was the rest of her staff, all of whom spoke less English than she did.

"Hi. We're the Smiths. We made a reservation from the States for the next two nights."

"What?"

"We're from the States. My name is Harold Smith, and I

made a reservation to stay here for tonight and tomorrow night."

"What?" (And I thought English was spoken in London!)

It took ten minutes to communicate who I was and what I was there for, and eventually to get her reply: "We don't have reservation. You have no room."

I should have had second thoughts about staying at Hungary-East right then and there. I could see Judy was already put off by the language barriers—not to mention the risqué posters hanging in the converted waiting room that now served as the bed and breakfast's cluttered office. (What my sons didn't know about the female anatomy, they learned while waiting for a room!) Still, we were in a foreign land, and I wasn't exactly sure what our alternatives were, lodging-wise. Moreover, I felt strongly that when in Rome, er, London, do as the Londoners do. I therefore stuck to my guns and somehow, twenty-five minutes into our lesson in rudimentary English, I secured a room—four floors up a narrow spiral staircase.

Our Hungarian host, perturbed because of "all the trouble" she had to go through to make good our reservation (which she eventually found), called for her maintenance man to show me the room (shades of my youth). He motioned for me to follow him into a service elevator that looked to be the size of a phone booth.

Needless to say, it was uncomfortable to ride four floors in the face of someone you had only just met. Our bodies were packed like sardines in the three-foot by three-foot by six-foot "lift." How close were we? Let's just say that when the sliding door opened on to the fourth floor, my shirt and trousers were permanently pressed!

The room itself met more of my requirements (it had beds), than Judy's. The beds looked clean (I assumed the sheets were naturally green, red, and brown), but they were literally right next to one another, making any movement all but impossible. Consequently, there was no room for our suitcases; and changing clothes was a task to be done only in the "hallway" between the bedroom and the bath. Speaking of the bath, it was, as we were to learn later, typically English, with a shower that only dribbled water. You could get your hair wet enough to shampoo it, but a thorough rinse was an hour's commitment.

Still, for all its shortcomings, it *was* a room. And my family *was* tired. So I took it.

As I walked down the stairway to the office and my family (I let the maintenance man go down the elevator alone), I proudly nodded to Jude that we had a room—and shook the keys triumphantly for my tired family to see. I could see, however, that Judy was only mildly impressed. She had a keen sense of place, and I was aware she knew this place was definitely not the Hilton.

"Honey," I said to encourage and convince my wary wife, "it's not the nicest room, but it has plenty of personality."

"Does it have running water?" she asked.

"Yes, it has a shower."

"Does it work?"

"Very slowly."

"And the beds?"

"There are two."

"Harold," Judy said, frustrated. "What was the name of that motel you stayed at when you were a kid that was so bad?"

"The National."

"Is this the English version of the National?"

"Absolutely not!" I countered. "This place has posters from the continent. An international staff. And an elevator." Which Judy and the boys promptly took—leaving me to carry five suitcases up four flights of narrow winding stairs.

Your "Perfect Vacation" Planner
Things to remember on the holiday road.

The amount of traffic you encounter on any given travel day will be inversely proportional to the time you have left before losing that night's motel reservation.

8

The Seoul of Miss Manners

SEOUL, SOUTH KOREA, 1986

Judy Smith, ugly American. Just the thought of it is grating.

Judy's number-one fear, the few times we've been fortunate enough to travel outside the United States, is she will be labeled with this epithet by some citizen (and having it happen miles away from the nearest U.S. Embassy). She's so obsessed with not offending anyone that before each overseas trip, while I'm reading about exchange rates and sites to see, Judy studies the nuances of the culture.

Did you know, for example, that you should never expose your palm when hailing a cab in Korea? It's like shouting an obscenity at the driver whose attention you're trying to get. (What obscenity, I have no idea!)

Or did you know you should never tip in Japan? No, not because they don't need the money, but because by tipping you are taking the joy of service away from your server and making him or her a mere hireling.

Judy knows these and ten thousand other subtleties that will supposedly keep her, and by association me, from creating an international incident ("AMERICAN TIPS WAITER. TOKYO DEMANDS

SANCTIONS AGAINST U.S."). The problem with all this hypersensitivity, however, is that veteran Road Warriors such as me have little patience for such penny-ante details. Not that I'm a cretin, mind you. It's just that part of any Road Warrior's job description is adaptability to any new surrounding, whether it be England or East L.A. Indeed, a Road Warrior knows how to be inconspicuous; and, if need be, he knows how to use his basic American friendliness and "aw-shucks" charm to work himself out of potentially embarrassing situations or to quell any anti-American sentiment.

A case in point was our trip to Seoul, Korea. I was covering a religious event for the magazine I worked for, and in the course of my assignment, I was invited (along with my wife) to visit a "house church" and to join its small "congregation" for a mid-day meal. I was delighted to accept on behalf of my wife and me and looked forward to some direct cultural contact.

Judy, on the other hand, while warmed by the welcome, was terrified by myriad cultural faux pas she was convinced awaited us. Almost immediately, she set to culturally cramming the two of us on the do's and don'ts of Korean etiquette.

"Now, Harold," my teacher began, "be sure you take your shoes off at the doorway. Don't walk beyond the hallway with your shoes on. Okay?"

"Sure, no problem."

"And be sure you bow to our host and hostess at the doorway."

"Right."

"And please try all the food. We don't want our hostess to lose face."

"Got it!"

"And be sure . . ."

"Honey," I interrupted, "I think I have the basics down pat. I'll just play the rest by ear. We'll have a great time. Trust me."

As we left for our first hands-on interaction with Korean culture, I was ready for a Kodak moment. Judy, on the other

"THERE MUST'VE BEEN A HUNDRED SIGNS!
'DON'T FEED THE BEARS!' DID YOU LISTEN?! NO!
YOU GO AND START PASSING OUT COOKIES TO
THEM ALL AND <u>NOW</u> LOOK AT US!"

hand, was ready to run interference for her etiquette-impaired man.

❖

Upon our arrival I interrupted our hosts in mid-bow with a hearty Midwestern how-the-heck-are-ya handshake, putting some extra feeling in it to clearly communicate my pleasure for being invited into their home. They may have momentarily thought I was an intruder trying to arm wrestle them into submission, but my wife's gracious bows allayed their fears. Score another "face-safer" for Judy.

We moved through the doorway and entered the dining area. About twelve guests sat cross-legged around the dinner table awaiting our arrival. Judy joined them, as I would have if I hadn't been so surprised that there were no chairs. Our hostess sensed my confusion and graciously offered me a couple of cushions as a "halfway" measure.

Sitting cross-legged for two hours is no easy thing, especially with leather shoes cutting into the sides of your legs. (Yes, I forgot to take my shoes off in all the bowing and hand shaking.) But in true Road-Warrior–style, I adapted by stretching my legs out under the table and only periodically rubbing them against the startled young woman who sat across from me. Thus situated, I settled in for a true Korean feast.

I was only beginning to learn about Korean cuisine, so Judy's exhortation to "try everything" was no problem. I moved through the "sticky rice" (a wonderful sweet rice that someone should tell Uncle Ben about) and *bulgogi* (Korea's version of barbecued pork) to the assorted fruits and, of course, the tea. Gingsing tea, to be exact—a strange, almost medicinal brew that tastes like steeped sweat socks. It is believed to make men more virile (if they can get it down), and can garner a pretty penny in nutritional and health shops outside of the country.

Desperate men do desperate things.

The meal continued for more than an hour, with new foods

being brought out every ten or fifteen minutes. I went overboard making Judy proud and helping our delightful hostess save face by sampling every serving and relishing every morsel.

The final food served before dessert was a clear broth with chunks of cabbage and red pepper suspended throughout. The hostess gave me a small ladle and motioned me (or I should say, my ladle) toward the bowl.

"What am I supposed to do?" I whispered nervously to Judy.

"She wants you to serve yourself, and then pass the ladle to me."

"But it looks like she's motioning for me to dip and sip."

"Well, of course she is," Judy answered. "You pour yourself the soup, then eat it."

"No sweetie," I proudly countered. "I think I'm supposed to eat this right out of the bowl."

"What!"

Ignoring my wife's exclamation, I confidently dipped the spoon into the bowl and drew it toward my mouth. Suddenly all eyes seemed curiously fixed on me—especially our hostess' (whose mouth opened wider the closer the ladle got to mine). Finally, I swallowed a hearty mouthful of the unidentifiable "soup," then sat back and smiled.

For what seemed another hour, nobody moved or took their eyes off me. (Probably because Judy *was* right: I was supposed to fill my bowl then pass the ladle on to her.) And for the first time during my cultural *tour de force*, I genuinely started feeling uncomfortable. The discomfort steadily grew as the toxic concoction I had swallowed started doing a slow-burn in my throat and stomach.

I later learned the "soup" was *kimchi*—the national dish prepared by putting cabbage, peppers, and anything else available into large, earthen jars and sticking them in the ground for as long as you can stand the smell. And believe me, that smell is everywhere.

Once again, our gracious hostess took pity on her visiting

ugly American and came to my aid with a glass of iced tea. Yes, it was iced Gingsing tea—but desperate men do desperate things.

I could tell by the look on my wife's face that she probably wouldn't be recommending me for state dinner duty any time soon. However, when feeling finally came back to my mouth, laughter had replaced the stares of all around me. I laughed as well, knowing that the *kimchi* had turned a potentially embarrassing moment for our hostess—the ladle in my mouth—into an embarrassing moment for me. To the delight of everyone.

Yes, the Road Warrior had once again claimed victory from the jaws of certain cultural defeat.

"Now," I said to our hostess with restored confidence. "Any dessert?"

YOUR "PERFECT VACATION" PLANNER
Things to remember on the holiday road.

"Deluxe," in motel parlance, simply means an additional $10 room charge for putting stale mints on your pillow.

9

How Not to Sail a Boat

CARP LAKE, MICHIGAN, 1986

I have this thing about being on water: I hate it. I'm the original "Chicken of the Sea"; and anything that moves faster than a fishing boat is cause for me to mutiny.

My dislike for open water—that is, anything you can drown in—was probably birthed in Delray Beach when I was five years old (see chapter 1). But if that early experience wasn't enough to create within me a negative attachment to H_2O, then riding in my grandfather's speed boat was the *coup de grâce*.

Grandpa Smith was not a Road Warrior in that he rarely ventured far from home. But home happened to be on a lake, which meant he would spend long evenings and even longer days racing between terror-stricken swimmers and water skiers, barely avoiding docks and buoys, and generally transforming this heavily developed resort area in southcentral Michigan into his own watery demolition derby. So fast would he gun his Mercury outboard engines that the front end of his boat would leave the water by a full four to five feet, leaving its passengers (sometimes eight or nine in his five-seater craft!) reflecting—with mouths agape—on the fragility of life.

(Grandpa's water-borne recklessness knew no bounds. During one winter, he drove me onto the frozen lake and promptly car-skated figure eights. When I asked him if he was sure the ice would hold us, he matter-of-factly replied: "Son, I'm not sure of anything!")

In all I remember going out in a boat with my grandfather about twenty-four times. And I remember enjoying the ride only once—the time we ran out of gas and had to row back to shore.

As you can see, then, my early childhood experiences with water were hardly positive. (No wonder I took Mom at her word when she said you could drown in a cup of tea and stayed clear of tea for years!) As I grew to adulthood, I did little to address, let alone conquer, this fear. Oh, I'd go to a beach—but only to get a tan. Swimming? Sure, if I could touch bottom.

Boating? Only if it meant getting to a great fishing hole.

And only if Grandpa was somewhere on dry land!

Speaking of great fishing holes, Carp Lake in northern Michigan isn't one of them. But it happens to be where Judy's family has had a cottage for over fifty years, and where the four of us go at least once every year to just veg. The kids dig in the sand. They build evening bonfires. They explore the nearby woods. And yes, they swim.

Judy and I, on the other hand, just relax. We watch the kids do all of the above while capturing a few extra-needed "Zs." Not a normal vacation for the hardened Road Warrior, to be sure. But a much needed break before our next storied adventure on America's interstates.

Joining us for our annual week of relaxation along the shores of this calm and quiet lake were our good friends, Ed and Debbie and their four kids. Ed, like Grandpa Smith, is not a Road Warrior. However, like Grandpa, Ed can be caring, compassionate, impetuous, and easily given to what some people might consider recklessness.

"Ed, are you sure it's safe to take your sailboat out on the lake in an electrical storm?"

"Harold, I'm not sure of anything!"

So into the lake we went (Grandpa Smith would have been proud)—Ed and I on a flimsy thirteen-foot sailboat that I didn't know the first thing about. And yes, there was a major summer storm moving in, and the winds were transforming the usually placid lake into a choppy, wave-tossed sea. What a way to start a vacation!

Why I said yes to Ed when he asked if I'd like to try out his new boat, I don't know. Perhaps I thought I could once and for all lay to rest the fear I had carried with me since childhood. Or perhaps, as Judy later suggested, it was sheer and simple stupidity. Whatever the reason (it was probably the latter), I was now huddling in the back of the boat (the stern?), wrapped in a life-preserver, watching Ed do all in his power to keep the driving winds from driving us under the water.

Ed is the kind of person who knows just enough about a lot of things to be lethal. Take sailing. He learned the basics by watching others and by asking other neophyte sailors such rudimentary questions as "What is a sail?" and "Where exactly is the rudder, and what exactly does it do?" By the end of his training (and a couple quick sails on tranquil waters), he determined himself ready to conquer all the aquatic world could throw at him—including a steadily intensifying electrical storm.

We nearly capsized at one point—and would have had not Ed showed some surprising skill in maneuvering the sails and the rudder to keep the boat afloat. I confess, my friend's moves and confidence were impressive and, for a brief moment, actually had me thinking we might live to tell about my maiden voyage. My hope, however, was short-lived, for another gust of wind collapsed our sails and turned the boat upside down in the water—leaving Ed and me adrift and alone in the middle of the lake.

Now, Carp Lake is neither the largest nor the deepest inland lake in the north of Michigan. But like any lake subject to severe crosswinds, it currents and waves can make navigation almost impossible. And as hard as we tried to get back to our capsized boat, the maelstrom pushed us farther and farther away. I was scared, frustrated, and angry that the ghost of my grandfather—manifest in my friend—was evidently about to get the last laugh.

But then, not even Grandpa would have been foolish enough to be out in a storm like this.

Thank God for life-preservers. While they are hardly a fashion statement, they do keep you on the right side of water—the oxygen side. After half-an-hour of bobbing up and down on the biggest waves and deepest troughs I had ever seen on Carp Lake, me and my "jacket" were still afloat. And my resilient preserver allowed me periodically to rest between frantic attempts to get back to the boat. After one of these rests I was finally able to muster enough strength to swim to the floating hull.

However, as I reached for something on our sunken craft to hold on to, my right hand grabbed an exposed end of one of the sail guide wires. It was like slamming the palm of my hand down on a two-inch nail.

I had had enough.

"No offense, Ed," I said, as I watched the blood cover my entire hand, "but I hate sailing. And what's more . . ."

I was about to pontificate on the benefits of knowing what you're doing before you do it when we suddenly heard the sound of an outboard motor. It was a boat coming to our rescue.

"Let's get the bald guy with the cut hand first," I heard one rescuer say. "He looks bad."

I took no offense in my rescuer's description. Besides, he had the wisdom and wherewithal to take me first—and let Ed enjoy the full measure of sailing in a storm.

After dropping me off at the cottage to be tended to by Judy, my rescuers went back for Ed and, unbelievably, his boat. Both were recovered, and neither the worse for wear.

As for me, my sailing days were over. Period. It was a fishing boat or no boat at all. So the next day I went to the local bait shop to buy a license.

Making small talk with the owner over by the cash register, I commented on the severity of the previous day's storm.

"Landsakes," she said. "It was a doozy. Two or three boats were caught in the storm out on Lake Michigan and sunk."

I acted duly impressed.

"And on this lake, two idiots tried to go sailing!"

I felt the urge to bring my collar up to cover my head.

"Really?" I said.

"Yeah," she replied. "Can you believe it? They were lucky to be rescued."

"Do you know who they were?" I asked, praying for anonymity.

"No. But they were from out of state. Can you believe how stupid some people can be?"

"No, I can't," I firmly said.

With that, I paid my fee and quietly slipped out of the store— never again to come within one hundred feet of a sail.

YOUR "PERFECT VACATION" PLANNER
Things to remember on the holiday road.

The bugs you collect on your windshield and grillwork will eventually come off. Then again, so will the paint on your car.

10

"Watch It Mister, That's My Wife!"

Travel not only allows you to show off your prowess as a Road Warrior, but it also affords you the opportunity to show off your wife, and boost your male ego a notch or two. If you're a guy, you know what I mean. You look and feel like country singer Lyle Lovett. Nobody pays you much attention, but add your own Julia Roberts to the mix, and *bam*, all eyes are on you.

I speak from experience.

When Judy and I visited Japan, for instance, people on the street would come up to Judy and tell her how beautiful she looked. Or they would touch her skin and tell me how lucky I was to be married to such a woman.

In England, people would comment on her "English good looks" or commend me on my selection of a wife.

And in Hawaii, one person was so taken by Judy's looks that he asked her out on a date—an experience that gave this Road Warrior about all the ego boosting he could handle.

We had arrived in Honolulu from Seoul, Korea, and spent three days sleeping off jet lag and circumnavigating the lush green isle of Oahu. It was now our last night and we felt obligated to do

IT WAS A CLEAR SIGN THAT THE MULBYS
HAD BEEN ON THE ROAD FAR TOO LONG.

what millions of other tourists had done—attend a luau and experience the "real" Hawaii. All for "only" twenty-five dollars apiece!

We readied ourselves for the evening's main attraction by shopping for "just the right" clothing. Judy bought a colorful, sleeveless dress, which accentuated both her beautiful figure and the dark jade necklace she had purchased in Seoul. I, on the other hand, felt the need to make a more dramatic cultural statement. (Although which culture I'd be embarrassing was never quite clear.) I bought a pair of khaki pants (no radical statement there) and a short-sleeved, black "Hawaiian" shirt with red, green, and pink floral print (plenty of statement here).

As we stepped onto the bus that would take us to the "real" Hawaii, our tour hostess immediately commented on our "real" Hawaiian look.

"The colors of your dress are the colors of our island," she graciously said to Judy. "It is very beautiful."

She then turned to me, trying to suppress a smile. (Or was it a laugh?)

"And your shirt, sir, is very *kamacamaca*" (or some such native description).

Both the bus driver and our hostess started laughing. I thanked her for the "compliment" and headed for our seats.

"Judy," I said rather disconcertedly, "our guide won't take her eyes off me."

"Harold, she's not looking at you. She's looking at your shirt.

"Is there something wrong with my shirt?" I asked.

"Not at all. I think the word is *kamacamaca*."

"That's not bad is it? I mean, you're not embarrassed to be seen with me, are you?"

"Harold, of course not! Besides, it'll be dark soon."

The "real" Hawaii may start at twenty-five dollars, but it gets costlier the more "real" you experience.

When we arrived at the luau, we were ushered into two lines, one for men and one for women. Judy got her picture taken with some twenty-year-old, loin-clothed, surfer-type; and I got my picture taken with some grass-skirted, halter-topped, hula-type.

"Remember your authentic Hawaiian luau: Only $10 a shot!"

Then there was the open bar. Being teetotalers, Judy and I got off Scot-free here, enjoying as many complimentary Cokes as we wanted. The couple next to us, however, must have been well into their fourth and fifth $5 cocktails respectively when the luau emcee finally announced that dinner was served.

Two or three tables at a time were excused to go up to the food tents and pile on as much food as their real Hawaiian paper plates could hold. It was all five-star—the roast pig, the corn, the pineapple—everything, that is, except the *poi*.

With the consistency of wallpaper paste and the taste of salted sawdust, *poi* is made from cooked taro root that is then pounded to a paste and fermented. On my list of foods to avoid at all costs, it ranks significantly above Korea's *kimchi* or Scotland's *haggis* (meat and oatmeal cooked in a lamb's stomach). It's so bad that it is served to luau guests in tablespoon-sized paper cups. From what I could see, it was the only luau food nobody went back for seconds on. . . . So much for the "real" Hawaii.

After finishing our first servings, Judy and I both decided to reload on the pork and pineapple. I told Judy to go first while I stayed behind and saved our table seats.

Five minutes later, she returned, her plate full and her face flushed.

"What's wrong, Judy?" I asked. "Bad *poi*?"

"No, Harold," Judy answered with an embarrassed smile. "I was just asked out on a date."

For a split second I felt that mature pride that only a man can feel when the woman he's married to draws the attention of another man. ("Nah, nah, nah, nah, nah. She's mine and not yours!")

Then I felt perturbed.

"What'd the jerk say?" I asked.

"He just asked if I'd like to join him after dinner because 'it's not right that a lady like you be left alone after a luau.'"

"What did you say?"

"I told him he was right. It wasn't right for a lady like me to be left alone after a luau. That's why I brought my husband!"

I wanted to see who my "competition" was, so we left our seats and headed back to the food tents.

"There he is," Judy said, pointing to the *poi* table and to a man who was young enough to be my younger brother. Okay, my son.

We walked toward the wife stealer's table—not surprisingly the least crowded of all the food tables—and the moment he saw me, his brown skin turned beet red.

"You one lucky man," he said, trying to assuage what he thought might be anger. "You one lucky man." And with that, he had the audacity to give us a peace offering of two more table-spoons of *poi*.

Now, I could forgive the man for thinking my wife was a single college coed just waiting to be hit upon.

But two more tablespoons of *poi*?!

The rest of the evening was anticlimactic. The hula dancers were fine, the emcee entertaining, and the ride home on the bus was, well, a ride on the bus. Total cost for the "real" Hawaii, fifty-five dollars (which included a five dollar tip to our hostess—who, as far as I was concerned, was very *kamacamaca*).

There certainly have been other places where we've gotten more for our money. But then, you can't put a price tag on ego boosting. And thanks to the "Prince of *Poi*," both Judy's and my egos were doing just fine, thank you.

Of course, my ego's been pretty high ever since February 16, 1974—the first of over seven thousand opportunities I've had to end my day with a "college coed" who just happens to be my wife.

Yep, me one lucky man.

YOUR **"P**ERFECT **V**ACATION**" P**LANNER
Things to remember on the holiday road.

The food you order today
at an expressway oasis is
likely to have been prepared
six weeks ago.
And reheated yesterday.

11

The "Real" Differences Between Men and Women

After twenty years of marriage and eighty thousand vacation miles, let me bravely fly in the face of political correctness and say unequivocally that men and women *are* different. How do I know? I know! Don't believe me? Then all I can say is, you've probably never traveled with your spouse in a fully packed car for more than a day.

Indeed, a subcompact filled to the teeth with suitcases, duffel bags, picnic baskets, coolers, toys, and oh yeah, people is an ideal medium for seeing the true distinctives of maleness and femaleness with crystal clarity—for coming face-to-face with that mysterious sexual essence that is part of the dust from which man and woman are made.

So listen carefully. I have traveled in countless subcompacts. I have seen this essence. I have seen it in our luggage. I have seen it in our climate control settings. I have seen it when we're lost.

And I have seen it at every rest area between Chicago and

Los Angeles.

Believe me, we are different!

Gender Distinctive #1: A woman will pack for every occasion, a man will make do with the shirt on his back.

I have to give Judy a lot of credit: She always looks great on vacation. And why shouldn't she? After all, she dutifully relocates her entire clothes closet into two or three hard-shelled suitcases that collectively weigh a ton. I, on the other hand, usually look good *after* vacation, having spent two weeks pumping and lifting these and other travel accouterments in and out of trunks, up and down stairways, and around and across expansive hotel lobbies.

As for how I look during vacation, let me put it this way. I look as good as two pairs of jeans, two T-shirts, and two sweat shirts will allow me to look. Not that I'm complaining, mind you. This amount of clothing is more than adequate for fourteen days on the road, and it can be packed in an average-sized duffel bag— with plenty of spare room for Judy's extra shoes.

Indeed, convenience is key to the male approach to packing. And conversely, inconvenience is key to the female approach. This latter observation shouldn't come as a surprise to any male who's watched his wife deliberate over what to wear, then determine she has nothing to wear, then decide on the first suit, dress, blouse, or skirt she originally pulled out of her closet over an hour ago. This is a tough habit to break, so why even think it could be broken on vacation?

A man, on the other hand, tends to grab the nearest thing on the bedpost, floor, or—only in rare circumstances—hanging neatly in the closet. No matter if he wore it yesterday or, for that matter, the last two days. If it's clean, it's cool. And anyway, who'll notice?

Well, actually, your wife will probably notice, which is why Judy is always trying to get me to pack a few more items of clothing when we travel—just in case we meet the president or something.

"If you wear that Michigan University sweatshirt one more day, I'll scream," is a refrain heard across America during the summer months. In fact, if it's June, July, or August, listen carefully. You might be able to hear it from wherever you're sitting!

Gender Distinctive #2: No matter what the car air conditioner is set at, a man will always be hot and a woman will always be cold.

When I was a kid, family vacations meant traveling excruciatingly long distances in cars that never—never—had air conditioning. Sweating was as much a part of the Smith travel legacy as rolling down windows and eating dust in our futile attempts to stay cool.

Dad always explained our lack of an air conditioner as a simple matter of cost. "Son," he would say to me while I whined in the backseat, "an air conditioner is just too expensive. And besides, it kills the gas mileage.

"Now," he'd continue, "would you rather be cool and comfortable or have enough extra money to go to Yellowstone National Park? Or Disneyland?"

That argument won every time. (Chalk another one up for the Road Warrior!) After all, I loved to travel—even if it did mean sitting in my own (and my sister's) sweat for three or four long-distance days on the road.

But today I know the real reason why my dad refused air conditioning: Dad knew—as I have also learned—that what is comfortable to a woman is anything but to a man.

"Honey, would you mind turning down the air conditioner," Judy says. "I'm cold."

"Okay." And with that I change the climate control to a temperature that should provide Judy the "warmth" she needs while keeping me cool and comfortable—let's say seventy-four degrees.

Only five minutes pass and Judy is again telling me she's

cold and wants me to set the in-car temperature a little warmer—to, say, seventy-eight degrees. I do, but this time not without verbalizing my concern that the car will become too hot.

Ten minutes later my concern about the car becoming too hot proves prophetic. I look at Judy, then look at the climate control, and find she's surreptitiously raised the temperature.

"No wonder I'm hot! It's eighty-four degrees in here!"

"But I'm still cold," Judy says, showing me a collection of goose bumps on her arm.

What to do? I love my wife. I certainly don't want her to be miserable. But what about my own comfort? Doesn't the driver get some consideration here?

Over the course of the next hour the climate control is changed no fewer than fifty-six times. The in-car low reaches sixty-six degrees, with highs in the upper eighties! Finally, neither one of us can take the shifting weather patterns any longer and we resign ourselves to doing the only thing left to do: We turn the air conditioner off and roll down the windows.

Boy, Dad was smart!

Gender Distinctive #3: A woman will ask for directions if she's lost, and so will a man—but only to prove he's not as lost as his wife thinks.

We've all heard it said that if any man gets lost, he will absolutely refuse to ask for directions. The reason for this behavior, according to conventional wisdom, is that an admission of failure is somehow a slap at male machismo, a strike against male self-sufficiency.

Nothing, of course, could be further from the truth. It's just that in asking for directions, we men would never want to communicate to our wives that we are not in control of the situation at hand. Their well-being, their peace of mind, may well be at stake!

I developed this excuse, I mean, insight in the Osaka, Japan, underground.

Osaka Station may well be the mother of all train stations. A massive underground complex serving literally hundreds of thousands of people each day, it is the travel hub for all of southern Japan. It is also death to provincial Westerners who foolishly think if you've seen one train station you've seen them all.

For starters, the directional signs are impossible to read. There's nothing in Japanese calligraphy that looks like the good ol' ABCs. Which means we English speaking-types have no idea which marker leads to what destination.

If that weren't discouraging enough, the automatic ticket dispensers are as "easy" as Japanese arithmetic. To this day, I still don't know how much money I spent on our tickets, or if we bought two round trip tickets to Nara, Japan (our destination) or two "unlimited mileage tickets" good for travel throughout the country for the month of September.

But the most difficult of all Osaka's challenges was the train selection itself. How exactly do you know what train leads to what city when you can't speak or read the language?

As I mulled this critical question over in my mind, I could see Judy mulling panic over in hers. Here we were, in a giant hole, ten thousand miles from home, waiting for a train with approximately half-a-million other eager travelers. Would we ever see the ancient city of Nara? Heck, would we ever see our kids again?

Finally, with Judy lost in her own desperation, I walked straight into a group of Japanese businessmen and asked if any of them spoke English.

"Are you lost?" asked one of the men in wonderful-sounding broken English.

"Not really," I boldly countered. "I'm just a little confused. Is this the track to Nara?"

"Yes," my angel replied. "It's the red train that will be here in a minute or two."

"See what I told you," I said, turning to Judy. "No problem.

We're right where we're supposed to be." And with that, we boarded the next red train.

Bound for Kyoto.

❖

Gender Distinctive #4: Men have better bladder control than women, except when the nearest rest room is three hundred miles away.

While male machismo is not the reason why men avoid asking directions, it is the reason why they determine to stick to the road hour after hour and, in so doing, avoid rest stop after rest stop. My dad, for instance, *never* made a potty stop for himself and, indeed, stopped for us only when we threatened to soil his new car's backseat.

Like Dad, I am obsessed with making good time and sticking to the four-lane highway come hell or high water. And while I am probably more sensitive to my fellow travelers' biological needs than the original Road Warrior was (I'll stop at least twice in a day's ride!), I am proud to say I am equally insensitive to my own body's infrequent calls for relief. Come to think of it, I am a model of control for all those who travel with me, a standard of perseverance by which my wife and sons' bladders can aspire.

Of course, the older I get the more willing I am to acknowledge that my wife may have something when she insists that it's wiser to heed nature's call *before* rather than *after* it becomes a cry for help. I learned this the hard way in the hinterlands of southern Wyoming.

In that breathtaking state, rest rooms are few and far between. Thus one afternoon when we happened upon one at a local dusty diner, my wife immediately took advantage of our good fortune.

Unfortunately, I didn't.

After a light snack (that included plenty of hot, steaming cowboy coffee), we left the cafe and set off for some bona fide desolation: mile after mile after mile of hills, mountains, and rugged plains, and all without any sign of life.

About an hour or so after leaving civilization, nature's clarion call hit me. I didn't feel it warranted any immediate action, so I kept the call to myself—although at the hour-and-a-half mark, it was clear to everyone that I was feeling some heavy discomfort.

"What's wrong?" asked Judy. "Are you sick?"

"No," I replied. "I'm just feeling that third and fourth cup of coffee."

"Well pull over. You don't want to get sick."

"No way. I don't wanna embarrass myself."

"Embarrass yourself?" said Judy. "There's no one here to be embarrassed by!"

My pride would have none of it, however, so we moved on. Another hour passed. I was now wringing my sweat-beaded hands on the steering wheel.

"Harold, will you please pull over. You're making me uncomfortable."

How embarrassing. But I reasoned that a soggy front seat might be even more difficult to live down, so I pulled over to the side of the road and waddled to a nearby ditch. Looking down both sides of the open road, I saw absolutely no one. The coast was clear.

The comfort I felt shortly thereafter was the stuff of legends. And indeed my satisfaction would have been complete had I not lifted my head and looked immediately across the barbed-wire fence in front of me. There, in full view, was a home. With front window drapes fully open.

And a family laughing and waving enthusiastically at their red-faced visitor.

YOUR "PERFECT VACATION" PLANNER
Things to remember on the holiday road.

Fewer and fewer gas stations actually sell gas. Instead, today's "super stations" fill you up on Cheetos, DingDongs, potato chips, and pop.

Section Two

❖

Like Father, Like Sons

12

Are We There Yet?

ANYWHERE YOU TRAVEL TO!
It's one thing to be adopted into the Smith legacy, it's quite
another to be born into it. It is with great pride that I tell you
our two sons, Andrew and Kevin, are even now—at ages fourteen and eleven respectively—preparing to take their rightful
places among the pantheon of Road Warriors past.

Imagine my excitement when I see Andrew gaze longingly
at a *Fromer's Guide to Anyplace* or watch Kevin joyfully flip
through a scrapbook with 1,093 pictures of "Our Trip West"—
and for the 1,093rd time.

It's enough to put a lump in the old man's throat.

Of course, I'd be lying if I said the thought of a cross-
country trip had always thrilled the boys. Truth be told, Judy
and I had to nurture their seedling wanderlust. We purpose-
fully created an environment in which their genetic sensi-
tivities for reading maps and getting lost could someday be
realized.

It wasn't easy. But passing on a high and holy legacy to the
next generation rarely is. What kept us persevering was our
vision of that day when Andrew and Kevin will look lovingly at

their future wives and exclaim for all generations:

"We're the Smiths, and we can do anything!"

Looking back on my sons' first travel steps, I can identify three elements in their vacation training that all parents would do well to emulate.

The wisdom behind the first element, *establishing a vacation vocabulary,* can be seen by any parent who has tried to answer the two questions any and every child asks when stuck in the car for longer than twenty-six minutes. The questions?

"Are we there yet?" and "How much farther is it?"

Answering the first question with a flat out "No" may be honest, but it is hardly satisfying to the questioner whose patience hangs in the balance. As for the second query, an answer such as "Another two hours" or "Another thirty-four miles" is equally dissatisfying, for time and space to a three-year-old can be measured only in the here and now. Not surprisingly, then, children make it a point to ask these same two questions over and over, hoping against hope for an acceptable response. Meanwhile, Mom and Dad dutifully answer each question over and over—hoping against hope that their patience will hold.

To avert the possibility of losing your temper and still give your child a satisfiable answer, I recommend you develop a vacation vocabulary that communicates to adult and child alike. For example:

"Dad, are we there yet?"

"No sons, we're not."

"But, Dad!" (Whine factor increases. It's time for the vacation vocabulary.) "How much farther is it?"

"Well, sons. Do you know how long the 'Barney and Friends' video we have is?"

"Yeah."

"And you really like 'Barney and Friends,' don't you?"

"Yeah."

"Well, we'll be there in about three 'Barney and Friends' videos."

"Yeah! We like 'Barney and Friends.' Hurray!"

Just how sophisticated this vacation vocabulary becomes is up to you. I know couples who have developed a Barnese lexicon to deal with any question pertaining to distance.

"Daddy, when's the next rest stop? I gotta go potty."

"Honey, we'll be there in the time it takes Barney and Friends to sing a song to Baby Bop."

"Mommy, how far is California from here?"

"Oh, honey, it's a long way away. It's like watching 'Barney and Friends' over and over and over again, today, tomorrow, and the next day."

And so forth.

Of course, the thought of "Barney and Friends" videos playing nonstop "today, tomorrow, and the next day" is enough to make the three thousand miles to California seem like a Sunday drive in the park—all of which underscores that the use of Barnese as a vacation vocabulary can be equally beneficial and satisfying to both parent and child.

After all, what adult wouldn't prefer three thousand miles to three consecutive days of "Barney and Friends" videos?

As you brush up on your Barnese, you might also consider a second element in the travel training of your youngsters—that is, *establishing an award system for good behavior.*

Coloring books and crayons, comics, and video games have all been awarded to Andrew and Kevin in recognition of their exemplary in-car behavior. The Smiths define "exemplary" as: (1) Not killing or otherwise maiming your brother; and (2) not asking either of two questions—"Are we there yet?" and "How much farther is it?"

The boys' good behavior is "reinforced" daily with one of the above prizes. In addition to catering to their natural materialism,

"OH, WAIT! I THINK I FOUND THE PROBLEM! I'VE BEEN USING THE NEBRASKA MAP INSTEAD OF THE VERMONT MAP! I ALWAYS GET THOSE TWO CONFUSED!"

this positive reinforcement helps maintain some semblance of civility in the car. That is, until the crayons melt all over the back seat or the one child with motion sickness reads his "award book" one too many times.

"Mom, I read my book."

"That's good, honey. Did you like it?"

"Yeah."

"That's great."

"Mom."

"Yes, son."

"I feel sick to my stomach."

"Just close your eyes dear and take some deep breaths. You'll be all right."

"Mom, it's too late. I threw up all over my new book."

I look around to see the damage. Yep. He's sick all right. All over the new book and his melted crayons.

I dutifully pull over and clean up the fruit of my son's exemplary behavior. Exemplary behavior that, in light of the awards given, I now define as:

- Not killing your brother;
- Not asking if we're there yet or how much farther it is;
- Not letting your crayons melt;
- Not reading your award book in the car;
- And above all else, not vomiting all over the backseat of my car.

Speaking "their" language, rewarding them for good behavior—these are critical in the vacation development of our children. But if neither of these politically correct, psychologically acceptable approaches results in the desired "travel love" you so deeply want to instill in your child, then I suggest a third element that I learned at the feet of the original Road Warrior: *Establish yourself as boss.*

You see, Dad didn't have Barnese to talk to us kids with. Nor did he have a lot of extra cash to positively reinforce our behavior. But what he did have was, "the word." And the word was:

"BE QUIET OR I'LL GIVE YOU A SPANKING YOU'LL NEVER FORGET!"

It wasn't "Barney and Friends," but it worked . . . every time.

YOUR "PERFECT VACATION" PLANNER
Things to remember on the holiday road.

❖

Myth #1 of vacation budgeting:

You can budget.

13

My Children, The Road Hazards

MESA VERDE NATIONAL PARK, COLORADO, 1991

Traveling with kids can quickly turn ugly if parents are not prepared for the "surprises" that invariably accompany children on the holiday road.

If you are not a parent, then consider the following to be a primer—some rules of the road for successfully traveling with your soon-to-come kiddies. But if you are a parent, then consider this a humble assurance that if you've had trouble maintaining your schedule and sanity while on family vacations—you're not alone.

It goes with the territory.

When traveling with children it helps to remember that kids speak their minds.

Children are naturally free of the inhibitions that characterize much of adult conversation. If, for example, something or someone annoys you, as a mature, socially sensitive adult, you keep the annoyance to yourself or until an appropriate time when you can get it off your chest and not offend anyone.

Children, on the other hand, have no concept of offense.

"Hi, Auntie Jean. You look silly in that dress." Or, "Hi, Uncle Jack. Are you really a bum like my daddy says you are?"

When on a vacation a child's freedom of expression usually takes the form of pronouncing negative judgments on something that you—the loving parent—have taken the last twelve months to painstakingly save and plan for.

When our family flew to England, for example, we had been in London only three hours when Andrew felt compelled to announce that he hated it.

"Why?" I asked.

"It's not what I expected."

What he had expected was wall-to-wall castles and knights walking the streets. What he got—up to that point, anyway—was city smog and traffic congestion. To Andrew, it was just like being back home in Chicago—minus the $7,000 in air tickets, hotel accommodations, rental car fees, food, and sundries.

In other words Cubs tickets would have been a lot cheaper.

After my initial hurt (and threatening to drop Andrew off at the U.S. embassy for two weeks while the rest of us "had fun"), I eventually took Andrew's comments in stride—and he eventually came to love England. But to avoid being the brunt of any verbal barbs in the future, I'll get a better fix on my sons' expectations before the next pricey adventure—and check to see if the Cubs are in town during my two weeks of vacation.

The second thing to remember when traveling with children is: Kids get sick at the worst times.

Neither of our sons has ever gotten seriously ill on vacation, but chronic ear problems have resulted in Kevin Smith's name being known in drug stores and pharmacies across the nation. His most famous prescription: one filled at the world-renowned Wall Drug in Wall, South Dakota.

Wall Drug stands as an ever-expanding example of the American entrepreneurial spirit. Its original proprietor and owner, seeing his prospects for financial success dwindling in the depressed economy of the 1930s, hit upon the idea of offering "free ice water" to hot and thirsty travelers making their way through South Dakota's arid landscape. The idea took hold, and more and more appreciative vacationers made it a point to stop by the drug store for free refreshment and to buy a few incidentals for the road.

But further cementing the store's popularity were its famous signs—distributed worldwide—listing the mileage to Wall Drug from nearly any corner of the world (including the Arctic!). Today, the combination of free ice water, five-cent coffee (a later concession for weary travelers), and worldwide advertising has resulted in a tourist-filled complex where the original Wall Drug is but a small part of a mini-mall featuring fast food, shoes, clothing, and of course, all the Wall Drug memorabilia the thousands who visit this landmark each year would care to buy.

We had just made the fifty mile drive from Wall (and Wall Drug) to Badlands National Park (see next chapter), and were preparing to climb some of the dried-mud mountains characteristic of the region, when Kevin started complaining of an ear ache. Sure enough, his temperature was 101 degrees, and Nurse Smith diagnosed her youngest son as having yet another in a long line of ear infections.

He was miserable—as I was when I learned the nearest and only doctor in this desolate region was back in Wall. So back on the interstate we went, to the pediatrician, and to Wall Drug to get Kevin's prescription filled.

All in all, Kevin's illness had us putting another one hundred-plus miles on the minivan and "losing" three hours of Badlands exploration time. It also had us leaving Wall Drug with an unexpected souvenir of $50 worth of antibiotics. Not to mention some free ice water to take his first pill with.

A third and final thing to remember when traveling with children is: Kids fight with each other. (If you have only one child, then read this rule as your kid fights with you.)

Even in a minivan, with one child on the middle seat and the other in the back, hands, arms, and legs invariably make their way into the other brother's space and "war" is declared. The resulting backseat noise not only diminishes your own enjoyment of the scenic splendor all around you, but makes you question whether you'll ever take the kids on vacation again.

However, there are effective ways to deal with sibling tension. Happily, as our boys have gotten older, a truce seems to have settled over the back two seats. There have even been times when our travels have seemingly brought the boys closer together.

For example, one day in Mesa Verde National Park we had spent the better part of an afternoon climbing in and out of cliff dwellings dug deep into the sides of the giant southwestern mesas. The primary means of reaching these archaeological sites are "kiva ladders"—or long wooden poles with wooden rungs.

We were making our way up the side of a mesa wall on one of these ladders when Kevin suddenly missed a step and tumbled down a couple of rungs—into the outstretched arm of his brother.

Everyone on the ladder below this unfolding scene momentarily held their breathe, then breathed a sigh of relief as Andrew held Kevin securely until an adult could lend him some support.

"Thanks, Andrew," Kevin said appreciatively.

"You jerk, Kevin, you could have been killed," Andrew "lovingly" replied. "Maybe next time I'll think twice before catching you."

"It's not my fault, Andrew, it's these stupid ladders. Anyway, I would have caught myself."

"No way . . ."

Judy, unnerved by Kevin's near disaster, soon joined the fray. She felt her sons arguing was ridiculous, especially in light of what could have happened.

I, on the other hand, stayed out of the argument altogether. After all, Andrew had seen fit to rescue Kevin, and in that one move had unwittingly assured me that, truce or no truce, there would probably be no future bloodshed in the back of the van.

So I let my three loved ones argue their way to our parked car and all the way to the next kiva ladder—confident that my boys really do love one another.

They just have an odd way of showing it.

❖

No matter where they are sitting, children will literally be on top of one another within the first ten minutes of your vacation. And you will literally be on top of them for the rest of the trip.

14

So That's Why They're Called "Badlands"

BADLANDS NATIONAL PARK, SOUTH DAKOTA, 1990
Call it a father-son thing, but I want my boys to look back on our travels together and remember me as one tough Road Warrior; a man whose wits allowed him to make the world—or at least the interstate—his oyster. A man worthy to be admired and, with the Smith legacy in mind, a man worthy to be emulated.

There's probably no better place for a dad to develop his reputation as a first-rate frontier father than the American West.

The American West. Rugged. Desolate. Not for the fainthearted or dull-minded. An environment that only a man's man would dare face. A hostile environment that only a man's man could conquer.

The American West, 1990-style. Just the place to show Andrew and Kevin my true mettle. It would be minivan against nature.

And so in 1990 we made our way to the foothills of the Tetons. We coursed the Snake River (this time without an electrical storm), and we explored sections of Yellowstone National Park far off the beaten paths. Through it all, I served as wise guide and leader, telling my family the history of each region and explaining the forces of nature that gave shape to all we were seeing.

Not that I naturally knew any of this, mind you. It's just that I was usually the one who was handed the informational literature when we entered each attraction. A quick read and, presto, I became the expert!

"Hey, Dad, what causes water to shoot out as a geyser?"

"Good question, son." With that I'd surreptitiously pull out the appropriate pamphlet, peruse its content, then turn toward my questioning son and deliver an answer that would make even a park ranger envious.

"Son, a geyser is formed due to the pressure created by tectonic shifts beneath the earth's surface, which, in turn, superheat the water.

"Gee, Dad, thanks."

"No problem, son."

With that, we'd move on to the next sight, the next question and answer.

By the time we got to Badlands National Park in South Dakota, I could only imagine how impressed—how proud—Andrew and Kevin were of their frontier father.

He's a Smith, and he knows everything!

If you've ever wondered what the moon was like but didn't have government backing to fly there yourself, then let me suggest a few days in the Badlands. Its crusty, dusty cliffs and pinnacles of dried mud eerily replicate a lunar landscape, as does the park's uniform color of grayish-brown. The only difference, as far as I can see, is the atmosphere, which in the Badlands is more suited to shorts and a tank-top.

We arrived in this other-world near the close of another hot July day. After checking into our motel, we eschewed our usual trek to the information center (*Who needs an informational "crib sheet" here? I thought. It's just a lot of dried mud.*) and set out to "experience the land."

THE FAMILY AT OLD FAITHFUL, TAKE 79.

We started our grand adventure at the "Door Trail," so called because of a narrow, winding passageway through two huge mud hills that leads to an endless vista of Badland mounds. We parked our van in a small, natural amphitheater a few hundred yards in front of the "door." Tall mud mounds surround the amphitheater's circumference, with one smaller mound smack-dab in the center.

Andrew and Kevin flew out of the car and made their way to the nearest mud mountain. Up the side of the amphitheater they fearlessly went, until they reached its summit—about one hundred feet in the air.

"Fearlessly" is the operative word here, for mud hill or no, one hundred feet up is nothing to sneeze at. One false step and it was a fifty-mile drive to the nearest doctor. Judy tried her best to caution the boys of the very real dangers of a slide down dry mud, but it fell to me, frontier father, to balance Judy's warnings with my own experience-forged wisdom on how—and how not—to become king of the hill.

Seeing this as a golden opportunity to instill awe and wonder in my boys for their travel-hardened dad, I carefully climbed the hill in the middle of the amphitheater, and from my muddy pulpit, I bellowed forth.

"Sons, thou shalt wear the appropriate hiking boots before attempting a climb of this magnitude."

"We know, Dad. Mom made us put them on before we came."

"Sons, thou shalt look for pathways made by earlier climbers before forging a new path of your own."

"We know, Dad. We basically took an old path to get up here."

"And sons, thou shalt always test your footing to make sure it is strong and true." I pointed to my own feet, gently rocking my body up and down to emphasize the importance of a firm foundation.

Andrew and Kevin were all ears by now—if only to humor their dad. And speaking of Dad, I felt something akin to a mountain-top experience, standing prophet-like before my worshipful throng of three. Here I was, instructing a future generation of Smiths in the ways of taming wild nature. Below me, Judy—looking up at her Road Warrior husband, at the pinnacle of his prowess.

"Be careful, Harold," she said. "I don't want to take three boys to the emergency room!"

I could only laugh at her warning. Perhaps she spoke out of a sense of jealousy. Perhaps she was wishing she was the one straddling the hilltop, that she was the one boldly instructing the flesh of her flesh.

Yes, it's hard to be humble when you're a Smith!

"See, sons. Secure footing. Absolutely essential." I was now jumping up and down, as if to put an exclamation point to this last climbing commandment.

"Yep, boys, absolutely . . ."

And with that incomplete sentence, the loose dirt under my right foot gave way, transforming my muddy pulpit into a fifty-foot mud-slide.

As I tumbled over the jagged rocks to the amphitheater floor below, I could see Andrew and Kevin running down their hill to come to my rescue (or maybe just to rub it in). I could also see Judy shaking her head in her when-will-he-ever-learn look.

When I finally came to rest on the amphitheater floor, my legs and arms were banged and bruised but happily not broken. Nevertheless, movement was difficult. Nurse Judy tended to the more noticeable cuts and scrapes, and prescribed a strong dose of common sense. The boys, however, were thoroughly impressed.

"Dad, Dad, are you okay?" they asked. "That was a cool fall!"

"Now do you see the importance of good footing, sons?" I sternly warned, as if the fall were an object lesson on their behalf. (Dads have to be "quick on their feet" in more ways than one.)

"Yes, we do, Dad," they replied, and then turned and headed for Door Trail. Their dad had looked the Badlands straight in the eye and survived . . . or had at least been clever enough to save face.

Judy, on the other hand, turned and headed for the car, confident that we'd probably need more Band-Aids and disinfectant before leaving this desolate landscape.

As for me? Well, I just stayed put, nursing my wounds, and wondering how I'd overcome my next challenge—getting up off the ground.

YOUR "PERFECT VACATION" PLANNER
Things to remember on the holiday road.

Visiting relatives is a surefire way to: (1) save lots of vacation money; and (2) find new motivation for getting to your next night's destination quickly.

15

Attack of the Killer Scorpion

SEDONA, ARIZONA, 1991

I admit it. By today's standards, I was raised in an "abnormal" home.

For starters, I loved my dad. Growing up, I thought he was the bravest, strongest man on earth. No, he couldn't fly like Superman (my other hero) and he arguably couldn't outsprint a speeding bullet. But leap tall buildings? Let's just say I wouldn't bet against him!

Whether he was "bringing home the bacon," resuscitating one of the cars, or playing catch with me on the sidewalk in front of our home, Dad was larger than life. And our annual summer treks to points near and far (usually very far) gave me a chance to see the Man of Steel in action.

One vacation memory especially captures for me the essence of this unflappable Road Warrior.

We were on our way out West (where else!) and were approaching Sioux Falls, South Dakota, on what was another run-of-the-mill travel day. It was nearly lunchtime, and my sister and I were looking forward to our first stop since early morning.

As we drew closer to our destination, however, the bright, blue mid-afternoon skies suddenly changed to a midnight blackness. In a matter of minutes, our uneventful drive became (at least to my seven-year-old mind) a life-and-death struggle. The heavens gave way and the rains came down in torrents, making visibility all but impossible. To make matters worse, the hurricane-force winds bent trees at near ninety-degree angles.

Traffic slowed. Then crawled. Then stopped altogether.

My sister and I were terror-stricken. Mom had the look of a condemned woman. But Dad? Nothing. Absolutely nothing. Just grim determination.

"Don't worry, kids," reassured our dad. "Just a little storm. It'll pass in a minute."

Translation? "We're the Smiths, and we can do anything!"

To this day I have no idea what my dad really felt as he drove through that tornado. I only know he was emotionless, taking the wind and rain in stride. As a result, his stature took on new proportions in my young eyes. We had survived because *he* was with us.

Wow! I thought. *Maybe he can fly!*

Which leads me to another little episode that occurred in the red rock canyons of Sedona, Arizona.

It was now me playing the part of "super-hero," and my cape and Man of Steel leotards had been in full view for wife and sons to admire throughout much of our first trip across America's Southwest. I had fearlessly walked through rattlesnake-infested fields in Amarillo, Texas, to give my oldest son, Andrew, an up-close and personal glimpse at a prairie dog metropolis. I had, Road-Warrior–like, confidently navigated flash-flood waters that had submerged the mountain road we were traveling in Santa Fe, New Mexico. And—as if I had anything else to prove—I had ruggedly subjected my body to riding the icy, natural waterslides of Slide Rock State Park in northern Arizona.

By the time we got to Sedona, that cape of mine was clean, pressed, and ready for action.

Wow, I thought, *maybe I can fly?*

It was our fifth and final day in Sedona. After eating a blazing hot Mexican meal in town (no problem for this Stomach of Steel), we made our way up a nearby plateau, at the top of which was our temporary "home." From the motel parking lot, we could see seventy-five miles in every direction. The sun was beginning to set behind one of the sandstone towers off in the distance, and its dying rays cast everything around us in a red hue reminiscent of schoolbook renditions of a Martian landscape.

It was breathtaking. I suppose the four of us would have continued watching in awe until the sun had completely set, had not Andrew's voice broken our mood.

"Whoa, Dad," Andrew yelled. "Look!"

"What is it?" I asked.

Before Andrew could respond, Judy answered with a shout: "*Scorpion!*"

Sure enough. Between our van and our motel room door—stuck in the doorjamb—was a nasty four-inch scorpion with an attitude. (I knew it had an attitude because of the hissing sound it made as we approached the doorway.) To make matters worse, it wasn't your typical scorpion. Rather, it was—according to a book Andrew quickly retrieved for proper identification—a Giant Desert Hairy Scorpion, one of the most poisonous scorpions in Arizona.

From this point on, there is some discrepancy among Smith family members as to what exactly took place next. Actually, two disparate views exist—mine, and everyone else's. But to ensure that truth prevails, let me briefly paraphrase both.

According to Andrew and Kevin:

"Dad chickened out. While Mom and us went after the scorpion with some rolled up newspaper, Dad stayed behind our parked car, asking us every few seconds if we had killed the beast. We finally wounded it and got it out of the doorjamb. It ran for some bushes. At that point, Dad ran for our motel room door."

Thanks, boys. Very flattering.

Now the real story.

It is true, I did stay behind our parked car. But not out of fear; I was assessing the seriousness of the situation. I felt that Andrew, who was twelve at the time and approaching manhood, needed to experience firsthand some of the same thrills I experience each day on vacation—that is, taking raw nature by the tail (figuratively speaking, of course) and showing it who's boss. Besides, I could see that Judy and the boys had the upper hand in this particular battle royal. Why spoil their fun?

Being the good sport I am, I let my family chide me for my apparent "cowardice." (It's not easy being a super-hero.) Kevin, bless him, even snuck a souvenir scorpion paper weight under my pillow, just to get another rise out of dear old dad.

Little did my skeptical sons realize that my restraint was solely for their benefit. Twelve and nine years of age is not too soon to train up a child in the ways of manly confidence, and they'll no doubt thank me someday for the lesson in bravery I allowed them to learn. When they are called upon as husbands and fathers to perform heroically in the face of danger, I want their families to look at them and wonder: "Wow. Maybe he can fly!"

So, content that I had helped my sons take a giant step toward their one day super-hero status, I rested peacefully during our last night high up in the red rocks of Sedona. But only after checking one last time for any remaining eight-legged beasts.

For Judy's peace of mind, of course.

YOUR "PERFECT VACATION" PLANNER
Things to remember on the holiday road.

Although you'll bring thirty cassette tapes with you for in-car entertainment, expect your kids to fixate on only one of them. Also expect it to be the one tape you can't stand.

16

What I Did on My Summer Vacation

THE WISCONSIN RIVER, 1991

One of the givens of American education is the question asked by every preschool and elementary teacher on the first day of classes: "Now tell me, what did you do on your summer vacation?"

As you might expect, growing up, I looked forward to being asked that September question.

"Whoa, Harold. You mean you actually went through a tornado?"

"That's right, Randy. Four-hundred-mile-per-hour winds and rain falling so hard that it cracked some windshields!"

"Were you scared?"

"No way!"

"Harold, did your trailer really break off from your car?"

"You bet, Cindy! For all we know, it may still be flying somewhere over the Canadian Rockies."

My response to the teacher's question was cinematic in scope. Whereas most of the kids answered with a simple "We went swimming" or "We visited my grandma," I would answer in Technicolor detail—and keep the "film" rolling for as long as the teacher could abide the plot.

❖

As long as teachers continue to ask that quintessential first-day question, then Andrew and Kevin should never be lacking in a 101 good scripts. And with that in mind, I would have killed to be in school the day they rolled out "Our Trip on the Wisconsin River."

Rated R.

It was early August, and about twenty of us—four families from the same church—decided to spend a Saturday canoeing down the Wisconsin River. We would rent six or seven "three-seaters" and journey a total of ten miles, stopping for lunch somewhere along the way.

It fell to me and a dear friend of mine, Gary, to work out the last-minute details with the canoe rental people. We listened intently as the woman behind the counter carefully showed us our river route on her navigational maps. I can't say I understood everything she threw at us—you know, stuff about cross-currents, rapids, backwaters, and so on. But Gary was there, and he had already exhibited more knowledge of this kind of thing than I would ever have. For example, he could identify a canoe when he saw one!

I probably would have zoned out during this navigational primer had our rental "guide" not pointed emphatically to what appeared to be the biggest bend in the ten miles of river we'd be on that day.

"Any kids in your group?" she asked, in a tone that convinced me the waters in this area must be completely verboten to land-lubbers like us.

"Yes," I answered. "I think we have eleven."

"Then you'll want to take extra-special care when you reach this bend."

What could it be? I wondered. And why was she so reticent

"COME ON EVERYBODY! EAT! EAT! EAT! WE'VE GOT EXACTLY THREE MINUTES TO GET OUT OF HERE AND ON THE ROAD TO OMAHA! IF WE AVERAGE 63 MILES-AN-HOUR THE WHOLE WAY WE'LL HAVE FOUR MINUTES FOR REST STOPS AND TWO MINUTES FOR FUEL STOPS!"

to tell us? Waterfalls? Wildlife? Man-eating perch? What?

"Well, you see," the woman haltingly continued, "on both sides of this bend are nude beaches."

So it is the wildlife, I thought to myself.

"However," she said, "the bathers tend to be quite a ways back from the shoreline, so if you keep your canoes dead center on the river, you shouldn't really see anything."

I asked our benefactor for landmarks that would help us identify—and consequently avoid—this adult playground.

"Well," she smiled, "if all else fails, just look for the native fauna. They'll be wearing nothing but a smile."

Before embarking, Gary and I called a quick meeting with the other adults in our group to inform them of this unexpected "danger." Our game plan would be just as the woman behind the counter had advised; and Gary—with river map in hand—would tell us when we were approaching the bend in question and when to paddle our canoes toward the center of the river. So as not to pique our kids' curiosity, we all agreed it would be best to keep this revelation to ourselves.

The Wisconsin may well be *the* ideal family river to canoe—nude beaches notwithstanding. The river is wide and generally shallow (although its currents can be surprisingly strong). There are also plenty of places to dock your canoe and explore the forests or just sit along the shore and enjoy great white herons, cranes, and—surprisingly—bald eagles.

By the third hour of our adventure, my canoe—with our younger son, Kevin, and his good friend, Steve—was in the lead, with Gary, his wife, Colleen, and Judy in the canoe a short distance behind us. We had still seen nothing resembling a nude beach, and my keen sense of direction made me wonder if perhaps we had already passed it. Moreover, the day was overcast and somewhat chilly—not exactly the best weather for nude bathing. So I couldn't help thinking that maybe the woman's warning was a false alarm.

I motioned to Judy that I was going to move toward the shore to find a place where our troop could have lunch. I could tell she and Gary were trying to yell something back in response—but between the talking of my two young companions and the sound of a constant wind blowing across the river, I couldn't make heads or tails of what they were saying. I could only assume they were telling me that lunch on the near shore was fine, so I headed for dry land.

As I beached our canoe, I could still hear the indiscernible yelling of Judy and Gary. Only now they were waving their arms as well.

Still not knowing what their problem was, Kevin, Steve, and I set out to find the perfect location for our picnic lunch. Which wasn't hard. There was plenty of fine sand everywhere; and just back from the shoreline, a gently sloping grassy field—ideal for a friendly game of football. Very picturesque. Perfect, in fact.

Finally, Gary's canoe reached our noontime nirvana, but the look on his face was anything but peaceful.

"Do you know what you're doing?" Gary asked.

"Sure, finding a great place for lunch."

"But Harold," Gary said incredulously, "you've landed us right at the nude beach!" And with a "look that a-way" nod of his head, he directed my attention to the aforementioned gently sloping grassy field.

Sure enough. There, sitting and standing around a couple of tents, were a group of happy campers—with not a stitch of gear on them!

"Listen everyone," I said to the rest of our troop now beached on *the* beach. "We need to find a better place for lunch. I'll explain later."

But, of course, the questions and complaints came fast and furiously—especially from my son, Andrew, and his canoeing partner, Philip.

"But Dad," pleaded Andrew, "this place is fine."

"Son, there's a better place just up a ways."

"But Dad," Andrew continued, "Phil and I are starved."

"There's a better place just up a ways."

"But Dad, what's wrong with this place?"

"Son," I finally said with my best birds-and-bees-talk look. "There are nude people on this beach—that's what's wrong. Now let's go."

"No foolin'. Hey, Philip . . ." Soon our entire party was laughing and scanning the grassy field. And Andrew and Phil were employing their bird watching binoculars on this new, rare breed of native fauna.

Once we had all embarked, I conceded my lead position to Gary—who, unlike me, really did know one bend from another. I did, however, take solace in the fact that I was probably not the first to have landed at the No Bikini Atoll. For as we ate lunch on yet another beautiful—and safe for families—shoreline, we overheard another group of canoers look our way and happily exclaim:

"Oh, *here's* where you eat lunch if you want to keep your clothes on!"

Three weeks later. The first day of sixth grade.

"Andrew."

"Yes, teacher."

"What did you do this summer?"

"Well, I probably saw more of God's creation this past summer than I have ever seen before."

"That's wonderful, Andrew. Why not share what you saw with the boys and girls."

"Well, I'd like to wait until next hour."

"Why next hour?"

"Because it's health class. It just seems more appropriate to share my summer vacation there."

As they say, family travel is an educational experience.

YOUR "PERFECT VACATION" PLANNER
Things to remember on the holiday road.

No matter how much money you spend on your vacation, your children's fondest memories will be the "scratch and sniff" stickers you gave them for being good in the car.

17

Wanted: Souvenirs— Dead or Alive

Vacations cost money. Lots of it. Your average motel room runs around forty to fifty dollars, and that's excluding air freshener and Lysol! (Yes, I know, camping can be cheaper. But remember, I like to have *fun* on my vacations!)

Food? Well, there's always Macs and Burger King. Or cheaper yet, Weenies-R-Us and Bun-on-the-Run. But the cost of all those Happy Meals adds up quickly. What's worse, those Happy Meal toys and day-old fries compound in-car clutter. So much so that by day three there's usually only room in your car for your luggage, the kids' toys, the kids' pillows, the kids' cassettes, and the kids' books.

Not, however, for the kids.

Then, there are souvenirs—those costly, space-grabbing, I-just-haveta-have-it items that are usually forgotten two days after you return home. Why are they so quickly forgotten? Because it is an unwritten law that "souvenir" and "taste" be mutually exclusive terms, thus paving the way for Old Faithful toilet seat covers ($17.50), crystal amulets from the red rocks of Sedona guaranteed to put you in touch with Shirley MacLaine

($65.00), and Elvis everything (costing mere pennies to thousands of dollars).

We've been able to avoid the lure of these peculiar conversation pieces. (Although I recall we did fall to the siren's song of the Jackalope—a manufactured stuffed rabbit with antelope horns popular in manufactured Western legend.) And truth be told, much of the credit for this kitsch avoidance goes to Andrew and Kevin. While certainly not above taking a longing look at a Grand Canyon pocket watch or a taco-chip Alamo with bean-dip mortar, the boys would much rather gather a "treasure" or two from the land itself than spend their limited resources at Davy Crockett's House of Junk.

Animate or inanimate. Living or dead. It doesn't matter. Just as long as it's free to take and it "memorializes" the land from which it comes. The souvenirs that fascinate Andrew are usually living, while the souvenirs that fascinate Kevin are dead. Long dead.

Neither classification of souvenir fascinates Judy.

Living souvenirs. These are specimens—usually no larger than your basic garter snake—of native fauna. Equipment for collecting such specimens includes some kind of capturing device (a baseball cap will do) and three or four glass jars, preferably of different sizes, to incarcerate the prize. Because they are less likely to break when "accidentally" dropped on a sibling's head, some parents prefer that their young naturalists use a coffee thermos instead of a glass jar. If you do this, however, be sure you have had all the coffee you need. Coffee with cream is bad enough. Coffee with Kentucky paper wasp is worse.

By the time he turned seven, Andrew had the art of capturing living souvenirs down to a science, blessing our travels with an assortment of bugs and small animal life. His crowning achievement was the entrapment (with a pickle jar and Saran Wrap) of two blood-red lizards from the foothills of the Smoky

Mountains in Brevard, North Carolina. Living on ants and small fruit flies lovingly supplied by their captor, these lizards traveled with us to Myrtle Beach and Walt Disney World in Orlando— where their glass playground eventually turned into a glass oven in Florida's sweltering ninety-nine-degree heat.

The lizard's lethal suntan underscores the problem with living souvenirs. They eventually die, and usually do so while you're still on vacation. This, in turn, leaves you with one sad child.

It also leaves you with one less souvenir to share your precious car space with.

I like living souvenirs.

I'm not sure, however, how I feel about the other kind of free souvenir.

Dead souvenirs are the skeletal remains of once-living animals—preferably "cool" animals such as elk, buffalo, and moose (the likes of which we don't see in Chicago). Ideally, these remains have been bleached white by the rays of the sun—a factor particularly critical if traveling great distances with these bones in a car in the middle of summer.

For reasons unknown either to Judy or me, Kevin began gathering bits and pieces of skeletal remains when we started going West on vacation. (Maybe it was all the Westerns he's watched featuring skeletal landscapes stretching across the wide, open spaces.) Whatever the reason, Kevin has built his bone collection into a natural history museum. Among its "showcase" items are the skull of a prong-horn sheep (secured in South Dakota), the horned-skull of a bull (from New Mexico), buffalo remains from all over Wyoming, and of all things, pieces of cow bones.

The episode surrounding these cow bones pretty much characterizes what you can expect if one of your own decides to "hunt" for the deceased variety of souvenir.

We were on our way to the rim of Capulin Volcano in New

Mexico, when Kevin spied some scattered pieces of "white" in the green fields to our immediate left and right. The more your son or daughter gets into finding skeletal remains, the more he or she will believe everything white at the side of the road is a skeletal remain. Over the last four years, for example, we've stopped for white Styrofoam cups, white disposable diapers, white paper towels, and so on. I was skeptical of this latest "find," but promised Kevin I'd stop on our way down from the volcano.

Which I did. And to my amazement, we were welcomed by a veritable field of dreams. All around us were picturesque cow bones, just there for the taking.

"Be sure to take only the bones that are completely clean," I told Kevin, who was experiencing a vacation version of Christmas in July. "I see some bones that still have skin on them, and we don't want those."

Kevin was in bone heaven! For fifteen or twenty minutes he and his brother gleefully gathered rib bones, leg bones, horns, and skulls. It was truly the haul of a lifetime. The fresh winds of good fortune had blown our way.

Unfortunately, however, those winds didn't stay fresh for long. Just a day or two out from Capulin Volcano, the van started smelling like a slaughter house. Our bleached white bones hadn't been bleached as completely as we had thought.

It can never be said that Judy or I have ever stood in the way of our sons' happiness. We feel it is vitally important to encourage our sons' inquisitive minds and to allow them to take a "hands on" approach to the wonders of the natural world.

Our rolling meat market underscored this parental commitment.

And so, to make the best of a steadily putrefying situation, we washed the bones, stored them in plastic, and at the end of each day, unwrapped them to dry in the evening sun. This daily regimen helped purify the air a little, but for most of the remaining three thousand miles, I could have sworn Andrew had captured a souvenir cow to go along with his assortment of lizards, bugs, and arachnids.

(What parents won't go through for their kids! I only hope they thank us someday for putting up with all this. Better yet, maybe they'll have inquisitive bone-collectors of their own!)

The moment we arrived home, the offensive souvenirs were removed from the car, unwrapped, and placed in a corner of our garage. The neighborhood dogs and cats loved them.

It's been three years now, and our garage still smells like the Old West. But then souvenirs are supposed to help you remember.

And believe me, "dead" souvenirs never let you forget.

❖

You will be ticketed on an interstate highway for going five miles over the speed limit because everyone else will be going too fast for the local sheriff to catch.

18

Just Say "Cheese"

When the Smith clan gets together, just saying words such as "National," "Cabela's," or *kimchi* is enough to transform a flagging conversation into an animated discussion on lethal lodging, giardia, or acid indigestion. But what's to keep the experiences behind "National," "Cabela's," and *kimchi* from becoming precious heirlooms lost in someone's failed subconscious?

The answer to this question is simple. As simple as one word: cheese.

Picture-taking is as much a part of the Road Warrior's repertoire as leaving early and driving late. It provides proof of his daring exploits and a record for future generations of Road Warriors to admire.

Today there is a plethora of camera types available and, as can be attested to by anyone who has had to view a friend's or family member's vacation pictures, a Road Warrior need not be proficient in the use of any of them. He or she simply needs to be able to identify and take advantage of the three major vacation "photo opportunities" (hereafter referred to as "photo-ops") that can transform run-of-the-mill snapshots into photos worth saving and showing—at least once.

Photo-Op #1: Family members by sign posts. State boundary markers are a wonderful way of proving to naysayers that you actually visited the states you say you did. Just pull off to the side of the interstate and take a picture of Mom and the kids tastefully situated around the "Welcome to West Virginia" road sign. Of course, doing this puts you at risk of getting a traffic ticket, since pulling off to the side of an interstate for something other than car trouble is illegal. However, if you should happen to be ticketed, ask the police officer present if he would be so kind as to stand next to the "welcome to our state" sign—thereby getting two memories for the price of one state infraction.

Photo-Op #2: Family member by scenic display. There's something about putting a family member in front of, say, Old Faithful that, to the photographer, makes the entire scene imminently more interesting. (If only to the picture taker.) Indeed some insist upon having a family member (usually his child or children) in front of every scene of natural or manmade beauty as if to salvage it from certain disinterest.

One man who carried this photo-op to new heights was . . . Grandpa Smith. Not a Road Warrior by nature, he did, however, happen to take a "trip-of-a-lifetime" to the Holy Land. While there, he managed to take no fewer than fifty-six slides of my grandmother in various poses in front of the massive Golden Gate along the walled city of Jerusalem. I vividly remember watching these very same slides with Judy and my great-grandmother (Grandpa's mother), and listening to Grandpa's running monologue, which—for at least fifty-six slides—was on perpetual replay:

(Slide #1.)

"Harold, here's a picture of your grandmother in front of the Golden Gate in Jerusalem."

"Gee, Gramps, that's nice."

(Slide #13.)

"Harold, here's another picture of your grandmother in front of the Golden Gate in Jerusalem."

"Yeah, Gramps. How long were you guys there?"

(Slide #32.)

"Let me guess, Grandpa. That's you and Grandma at the Golden Gate in Jerusalem."

"That's right, Harold."

(Slide #56.)

"Wow. Here's another shot of me and Grandma in front of the Golden Gate in Jerusalem."

This time, no response. We were all asleep.

Photo-Op #3: Family members only. Unlike photo-op #2, which features family plus point-of-scenic-interest, this photo-op clearly and simply puts family front and center. This is an especially popular photo-op when the purpose for going to a particular destination is to be with family and to enjoy—or at least try to enjoy—each other's company.

This was the case when we vacationed at the Lapham family cottage in Carp Lake, Michigan, when Andrew was three months old. Both Judy's mother and grandmother were visiting the cottage at the time, giving this particular visit the added dimension of having four generations under one roof.

Needless to say, a family picture was in order. It was a magic moment—a memory to freeze in time.

Judy asked one of her great aunts (another Lapham who happened to be visiting the cottage at the time) to take the historic picture. She nervously said she would—although the way she curiously fidgeted with the camera seemed to indicate she had never seen one before.

We all stood smiling along the lakefront in front of Judy's aunt, Judy holding a surprisingly sedate Andrew, who somehow understood the significance of this auspicious moment.

"What do I look through?" Judy's aunt asked, looking desperately for the Instamatic's viewfinder.

I momentarily pulled out of the line of smiling faces to show her.

"What do I push to take the picture?"

"I'M SORRY, MA'AM, BUT I'M AFRAID YOUR HUSBAND DOESN'T QUALIFY AS A CARRY-ON ITEM."

I again pulled out of the line of smiling faces to show her.

"Okay," she said. "I think I'm ready to take the picture. Say 'cheese.'"

"Chhheeeeeessse."

Click. In a split second, history was captured for generations to come. We thanked Judy's aunt for overcoming her nervousness enough to master the complexities of Instamatic photography. We assured her that her work would undoubtedly result in a photo everyone present would want a print of.

"No problem, kids," she graciously said. "I think you'll like what I took. I got all of you."

And true to her word, she did indeed get "all" of us.

Eagerly flipping though the roll of developed prints, we finally came to the picture we had so looked forward to seeing. There, for future generations of Smiths and Laphams to admire were a half dozen adults and one child—all visible from the waist down.

Yes, Judy's aunt had captured four generations of legs.

❖

Every souvenir shop will have a sculpted bust of Elvis handmade by the locals of the region's most-plentiful natural resource.

19

Like Father, Like Sons

OXFORD, ENGLAND, 1993
At forty-three years of age, I've already begun reflecting back on my life—taking note of my progress as a husband, a father. A man. Have I spent enough time with my family? Too much time at work? Do I need more exercise? Less ice cream? Am I satisfied with my accomplishments? Have I used my abilities wisely?

Have I prepared Andrew and Kevin to assume the heady title of Road Warrior?

I realize the answers to these questions will not be completely known until after I'm, well, vacationing permanently somewhere in the heavenlies. Still, I'm looking for a sign here, a sign there, that indicates either progress or the need for midcourse correction. Weight gain? Then I'll cut back on the peanut butter chocolate ice cream. Judy can't remember my first name? Then I'll try to take on fewer assignments (like this book).

Andrew and Kevin, Road Warriors?

Well here, I'm pleased to report, the "signs" are all quite encouraging. Indeed, this may well be the one area where—at half-life—I'm actually "ahead of schedule."

Two "signs" in particular give me confidence that the Smith

legacy will be in good hands for at least another generation. The first of these was sighted in Yellowstone National Park.

It was our first visit as a family to this grandfather of all U.S. parks, and we eagerly looked forward to exploring its eerie, volcanic splendor. Our accommodation was one of the Old Faithful "snow cabins," a no-frills log box about the size of your average half-bath. Our luggage alone made movement inside this two-by-four almost impossible. We were resigned to use the lone double bed as a throughway for getting from one side of the room to the other.

None of this bothered the boys. They were in the wilderness and our claustrophobic cabin simply accentuated the rustic nature of this rustic land. Indeed, Andrew and Kevin—ages ten and seven at the time—wanted to experience the park fully (a strong indicator of prospective Road Warriors). Within the first ten minutes of unpacking, they were not only experiencing it, they were tasting and feeling it as well.

"Hey, guys. How'd you get your pants wet?" I asked, still trying to arrange a clear passage in our cabin.

"We fell into the river," Andrew said, quite proudly as I recall.

"You what?"

"We fell into the river. We explored the other side of the river and were coming back when we fell off our log bridge and got wet."

"You what?" Judy joined in.

"We explored the other side of the river," repeated Kevin. "It was cool. Little geysers, boiling pools, and mud pots. I think we saw a buffalo. It was cool."

At this point, Judy gave me one of her they're-your-sons-so-what-are-you-going-to-say-to-them looks.

"Boys," I said in my best frontier father voice, "just be careful. This isn't Disney World. There are things here that can hurt you."

Evidently my words weren't the ones Judy wanted me to share with Andrew and Kevin. She wanted some boundaries established.

Some checks and balances that would allow for fun and adventure but ensure safety and survival. I could appreciate her concern, of course. But not being genetically a Road Warrior, she simply couldn't understand the male need to take control of a new environment; nor could she relate to the innate sixth-sense we have when it comes to dealing with all that nature can throw at us. To set her mind at ease, however, I told the boys I'd join them on their next exploration of the A-K Geyser Basin (so named by its discoverers, Andrew and Kevin Smith), which was about to embark.

When we got to the river bank, the boys showed me how they had navigated across by walking on an assortment of fallen logs and beaver dams. *All very ingenuous,* I thought. *Worthy of true Smiths.* I followed their lead to the other side, and found the "treasure trove" they had so excitedly told us about only moments before. It was a desolate spot—surprising since our cabin, and others like it, were no more than five minutes away. But the lack of walkways and other signs of civilization made us feel like we were walking on undiscovered territory.

We spent about an hour going from geyser to hot spring to molten mud pot, muttering an assortment of "oohs" and "ahhs." The care with which my sons walked across the delicate volcanic crust was impressive. But then, they had a second-generation Road Warrior to learn from.

When we finally returned to our cabin, we were eager to tell Judy all about our adventure. And Judy was excited about hearing every detail—not to mention pleased that this time her sons had returned to her dry.

"But Harold," Judy said, with only a tinge of sarcasm, "what happened to you?"

"I fell into the river."

Like father, like sons.

Three years later, a second "sign" of passage was sighted in Oxford, England. On the River Thames.

It was a lazy Sunday afternoon and Andrew, along with two friends, decided to inflate a rubber dingy and explore England's historic waterway. It was a solemn moment as they lowered their craft into the slightly polluted river. I couldn't help but think about all this hallowed channel had been witness to over the centuries . . . over the millennia. Romans. Vikings. Saxons. Normans. Now Smiths. If only this river could talk! It was all very humbling.

Can we have a moment of silence, please?

The three explorers fidgeted themselves into position (no easy task in a two-man dingy), then set out for their English adventure. Judy and I decided to walk along the bank just in case the expedition ran into technical difficulty.

Dodging tour boats and pleasure crafts, the boys showed themselves both capable and confident. So much so, in fact, that they decided to row over to a small lock in front of which the tranquil Thames turned decidedly more agitated for a hundred feet or so. It was a fitting challenge for so excellent a crew.

Entering at a point where they could experience the full force of the water surging from the lock, the boys rocketed down the length of the rapid with all the appropriate whoops and screams befitting their age. Once the ride was over, they rowed themselves back to the lock—and rode the rapid again.

I was impressed. My own seafaring exploits, limited primarily to a number of biteless fishing expeditions and one near-death experience in a thirteen-foot sailboat, have left me less than enthusiastic about being anywhere near water. Yet here was my oldest son controlling a flimsy inflatable raft with the same confidence I feel behind the wheel of a steel minivan with seat belts and air bag. These young people!

After their third ride down the rapids, they seemed to have had enough and prepared to row back in our direction. From where we were standing, however, it looked as though the threesome was suddenly having an unusually difficult time maneuvering their rubber craft. And the more we watched, the more difficult their progress was becoming.

"What's wrong, Andrew?" I yelled across the river. But Andrew and his companions appeared too busy to respond. Indeed, they *were* too busy—bailing water.

As we were later to learn, the last rapid run had driven the dingy into some hanging tree branches which, in turn, opened up three small holes on one side of the craft. Frankly, I would have panicked (air and water are not Road Warrior favorites). But our three adventurers quickly assessed the situation (these were slow leaks—they could get back safely) and slowly, steadily brought the boat to the other side of the river amid their non-stop laughter.

When it finally reached us, the dingy was more than half deflated. As for the boys? They were wet, happy, and full of harrowing stories of how they had bettered the Thames.

As for me—I was proud. Andrew had acted gallantly, I thought, in a manner worthy a Smith. He was not just a Road Warrior in genetic makeup, but a Road Warrior in deed as well.

The same, of course, can also be said about Kevin—although being three years younger than Andrew means he has three years less experience conquering the great outdoors. But what the young lad lacks in experience, he more than makes up with his confidence and self-reliance. And why wasn't he a part of the "Death by Dingy" adventure? Simple! Not exciting enough.

"Dad, it has to be white-water rafting or nothing at all!"

It makes a middle-aged Road Warrior proud.

YOUR "PERFECT VACATION" PLANNER
Things to remember on the holiday road.

You know you're approaching your final vacation destination when the skies suddenly turn threatening and the five-day forecast calls for "unseasonably" (pick one) cold, wet, or humid weather.

20

Reunion of
the Road Warriors

BRECKENRIDGE, COLORADO, 1992
It had all the earmarkings of an unforgettable two weeks. A Road
Warrior reunion.

Andrew, Kevin, Judy, and I would link up with the original
Road Warrior and Navigator for two weeks in the Colorado
Rockies. Our base of operations would be Breckenridge, nestled
between snow-covered mountains shooting eleven, twelve, and
thirteen thousand feet into the air. Itself 10,800 feet above sea
level, Breckenridge is breathtaking, rugged, desolate, and dan-
gerous—an ideal location for the "holy grail" of all Road Warriors,
the perfect family vacation.

Making memories mano a mano. Oh, be still my beating
heart!

Due to scheduling conflicts, Dad and Mom would be unable
to travel with us by car across the Iowa and Nebraska corn belts.
Instead, they would join us in Denver, by way of Stapleton
Airport. Leaving by car from Chicago, we therefore planned to
pick them up at the airport (Dad and I determined the exact
time), then travel the remaining seventy or so miles to our mountain paradise.

One characteristic of a Road Warrior I haven't talked much about is his extraordinary sense of timing. For example, I remember my father taking great pride at the beginning of each day "guesstimating" at what time we would arrive in various locations. More often than not—honestly about 95 percent of the time—he was dead on, give or take five minutes. The errant 5 percent was usually due to construction, traffic, or one too many potty stops. ("Kids, if you want to get to . . . [fill in the blank], then tomorrow no potty stops!")

Needless to say, such time mastery has stood as a model for me, and like my mentor, I pride myself in predicting times of arrival. So when Dad and I determined that the Stapleton pickup would be at seventeen hundred hours (5:00 p.m. for you lay people), the expectations were perfectly clear—we would indeed be there at seventeen hundred, come hell or high water.

It was a challenge accepted and a challenge met. For at 16:58, our van drove up to the United terminal.

"Well done, son," my father said, as he loaded luggage into the back of the van. "It's almost 17:00 right on the button."

The six of us spent the first two days in Breckenridge scoping out the countryside, oohing and ahhing at the majestic granite spires all around us. On day three, however, we decided to get a little dirty and do some mountain biking.

For the uninitiated, the primary difference between mountain biking and biking around your neighborhood is cost. Mountain bikes (which look every bit like those cheap balloon-tire bikes you see at Wal-Mart) can run anywhere from $1,000 to $4,000! Which is ludicrous when you figure the mountain biking paths in and around Breckenridge are paved—just like your neighborhood street.

Still, the breathtaking scenery makes the experience worth the exorbitant rental fees, and so Judy, Andrew, Kevin, and I donned our helmets and set off for Frisco, another hamlet about ten miles from Breckenridge. Mom and Dad decided not to join us on this expedition, preferring a good hike to trusting what is, to a Road Warrior, a suspicious mode of transportation.

We had been on our mountain bikes for only twenty minutes or so, when a chipmunk startled Andrew by scampering directly into the path of his oncoming front tire. Showing the control so characteristic of a Road Warrior, he immediately applied his brake and missed this road hazard by an inch or two. Unfortunately, only an inch or two behind Andrew's rear tire was his mother, who was oblivious to what was going on immediately in front of her. When she finally realized Andrew's bike was stationary, it was too late. She tried to stop, but in so doing, catapulted herself over her handlebars and onto the gravel at the side of the road.

By the time I came to Judy's aid (I had been well in front of the accident scene), she was busily trying to diagnose the multiple pains in her right arm.

"I think it's broken, Harold," she said.

"Can you move it?" I asked.

"A little."

"Then it's probably okay."

I should point out that unlike my wife, who is a registered nurse, I have absolutely no medical knowledge. Like my father before me, I simply assume all is okay unless you see lots of blood or the victim has passed out. Then—and only then—do you call a doctor.

After ten or fifteen minutes of trying an assortment of movements, Judy said we should be able to continue our ride. (What a woman!) We did—doing an additional fifteen miles to near Frisco and back.

When we rejoined my folks later that afternoon, Judy was careful not to focus undue attention on her increasingly agonizing injury. She well knew the Smiths just grin and bare pain, and the last thing she wanted in the midst of so many travel legends was to be considered a wimp. But by next morning, the pain was too much. She needed to see a doctor. Immediately.

I consented, of course, even though I hadn't seen any blood

THE WILSONS AND THE FEGLEYS LEARN THE HARD WAY THAT THE 20 BUCKS EXTRA THEY PAID FOR A ROOM WITH A VIEW AT THE WILSHIRE HOTEL ISN'T WORTH IT.

and Judy didn't look like she was ready to pass out. But sure enough, the doctor only needed to look at her arm to diagnose a severe elbow break.

It was now my turn to feel faint. The bill for casting the break came to $400, payable at time of services rendered.

And have a nice day.

In all my travels, both as a child and as an adult, a Smith had never experienced injury. A few bumps and bruises naturally. Maybe a scratch. But nothing necessitating a doctor's visit. And most certainly nothing costing us four hundred vacation dollars. On the contrary, we had always taken on the worst nature could throw at us—and won.

We're the Smiths, and we can do anything.

But now this. A broken arm. While I felt bad for Judy, I felt worse for me, for the pall this break had cast over the family legacy.

Judy must have sensed my embarrassment because she determined not to let a little discomfort wrapped in itchy, white fiberglass keep her from experiencing Colorado to the fullest. And to prove her point, she hiked step for step with me around the rocky high country of Mesa Verde National Park—step for step, that is, until severe leg cramps forced me to the ground.

"What's wrong with you?" Judy asked.

"Oh, nothing," I said, trying to save face, "just looking into the canyon."

"Yeah, right," she replied, then reached out to me with her one good arm.

"Here, let me help you up, old man," she said. My embarrassment was complete.

Hobbling to where my parents now sat waiting for their invalid son and daughter-in-law, my confidence as a legacy bearer was beginning to wear thin. I would have to admit that the rugged pathway had simply gotten the better of me, and that we had to cut our hiking excursion short. As I was about to make my confession known, my mother whispered to me that Dad—

the original Road Warrior himself—had hurt his back ducking under one of the lodge pole pines.

"We need to move ahead, carefully," my mother warned, "and get back to the car as soon as possible."

"So Smiths aren't invincible," Judy said wryly to her still-cramped husband. "I feel right at home."

"True," I said proudly. "We may not be invincible. But we'll never admit it."

For the rest of the walk—save for intermittent moans and groans from Road Warriors I and II—we didn't admit anything.

Other than we felt great. And that we were having a wonderful time.

Your "Perfect Vacation" Planner
Things to remember on the holiday road.

Whatever you do, always maintain perspective. And remember that even your most frustrating travel experiences may someday make it into print.